MW00678288

A
FIELD GUIDE
TO
MONTANA FISHES

Second Edition

Revised by
GEORGE D. HOLTON
HOWARD E. JOHNSON

Dave Books • Editor

Bev Veneziano and Donita Sexton • Design and layout

Glenn West • Color paintings (which are also reproduced in black and white)

Harold (Rich) Stevenson • Black and white paintings and line drawings
unless otherwise indicated

Bev Veneziano and Daniel Stinson • Map graphics

Produced by
Montana Fish, Wildlife & Parks
1420 E. Sixth Avenue
Helena, Montana 59620

Distributed by
Montana State Parks and Wildlife Interpretive Association
P.O. Box 9211
Helena, Montana 59604

1996

Library of Congress Cataloging-in-Publication Data

Holton, George D., 1920-
A field guide to Montana fishes / revised by George D. Holton,
Howard E. Johnson. -- 2nd ed.
p.   cm.
Includes bibliographical references and index.
ISBN 1-56044-479-7 (pbk.)
1. Fishes--Montana--Identification.   I. Johnson, Howard E., 1935-
. II. Montana. Dept. of Fish, Wildlife and Parks.   III. Title.
QL628.M9H65   1996
597.09786--dc20   96-17534
                                                           CIP

Printed by Advanced Litho Printing
Great Falls, Montana

CONTENTS

DEDICATION

To the memory of Dr. C. J. D. Brown, mentor and friend, fisheries professor at Montana State University, author of *Fishes of Montana.*

PREFACE

This field guide is intended to provide a concise, easily understood handbook for identifying Montana fishes. Changes from the 1990 edition include deletion of the Coho Salmon, which is no longer planted, and addition of the Central Mudminnow, which is now established. As this edition goes to press, 86 species in 21 families are known to be in state waters (including the Shorthead Sculpin which may be a variant of the Mottled Sculpin). In addition to these species, three unusual hybrids are described: the Northern Redbelly Dace x Finescale Dace, the Tiger Muskellunge, and the Tiger Trout.

Information on characteristics, habitats, and spawning seasons of the fishes was gleaned from many publications and augmented with observations by the authors plus numerous suggestions from fisheries personnel of Montana Fish, Wildlife & Parks and other agencies. Dr. William R. Gould, Professor Emeritus, Biology Department, Montana State University, and Dr. Reeve M. Bailey, Curator Emeritus of Fishes, Museum of Zoology, University of Michigan, were particularly helpful.

Designation of individual species as native or introduced and descriptions of native ranges are based, as a starting point, on information in C.J.D. Brown's *Fishes of Montana* (Big Sky Books Bozeman, 1971) and supplemented by other literature.

The range maps were initially prepared using maps from *Fishes of Montana* enhanced with information from Montana Fish, Wildlife & Parks' stream and lake databases. These were updated for this edition with information from field personnel, department databases, and the fish collection at Montana State University.

Models for the black and white fish paintings were taken from a number of publications however, *Handbook of Fishes of Kansas* by Frank B. Cross (Univ. of Kansas Mus. of Natur. Hist., Misc. Publ. 45, 1967) and *Fishes of Montana* were the primary sources.

We are indebted to the many individuals who assisted in preparation of this guide and to the authors of the many books and articles from which much of the information was selected Space limitation prevents individual recognition but we are sincerely grateful.

We hope this field guide is useful. To facilitate future revisions, the text is in a desktop publishing file. Please send corrections, new information, and suggestions to: Fish ID Guide, Montana Fish, Wildlife & Parks, 1420 East Sixth Avenue, Helena, MT 59620.

George D. Holton
Howard E. Johnson

Helena, Montana
July 1996

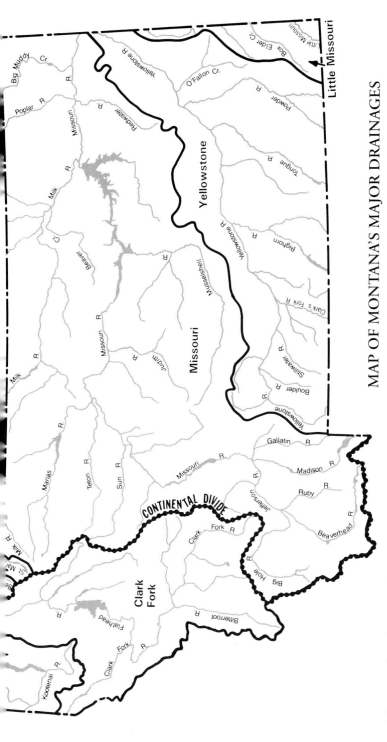

MAP OF MONTANA'S MAJOR DRAINAGES

Montana is the only state with headwaters of rivers flowing to the Gulf of Mexico, Hudson Bay, and the Pacific Ocean. Waters from the Missouri, Little Missouri, and Yellowstone rivers reach the Gulf of Mexico by way of the Mississippi River; the Belly and Saint Mary river drainages are headwaters of the South Saskatchewan River Drainage and flow to Hudson Bay through the Saskatchewan-Nelson river system; and water from the Kootenai River and Clark Fork reach the Pacific Ocean via the Columbia River.

The Continental Divide has separated westward-flowing and eastward-flowing waters for millions of years and has had a major influence on the distribution of fishes.

VISUAL KEY TO FISH FAMILIES

This is a visual key to the arrangement of fishes in this book. Families are aligned according to the type and position of fins on the back.[1] Use the drawings to determine which family or families a fish could be in, then go to pages indicated for descriptions of family members. In the text, look-alike fishes are generally grouped.

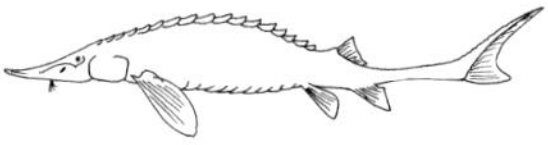

STURGEON FAMILY
pp. 15-17

PADDLEFISH FAMILY
p. 18

GAR FAMILY
p. 19

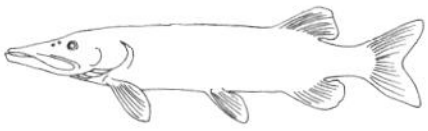

PIKE FAMILY
p. 20

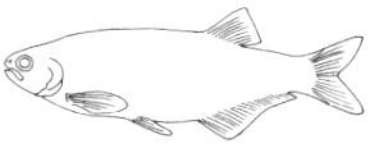

MOONEYE FAMILY
(Goldeye)
p. 21

SUCKER FAMILY
(Redhorse, Suckers,
Buffalos)
pp. 22-26

MINNOW FAMILY
(Carp, Chubs, Daces,
Squawfish, Peamouth,
Minnows, Shiners)
pp. 27-42

MUDMINNOW FAMILY
P. 43

KILLIFISH FAMILY
p. 44

LIVEBEARER FAMILY
(Mosquitofish,
Tropical Aquarium
Fishes)
pp. 45-47

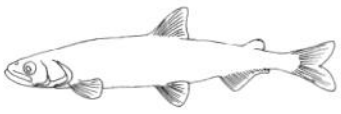

SMELT FAMILY
p. 48

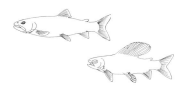

TROUT FAMILY
(Salmons, Trouts
Grayling, Whitefishes)
pp. 57-71

**TROUT-PERCH
FAMILY**
p. 72

BULLHEAD CATFISH FAMILY
(Catfishes, Bullheads)
pp. 73-75

CODFISH FAMILY
(Burbot)
p. 76

STICKLEBACK FAMILY
p. 76

SUNFISH FAMILY
(Crappies, Sunfishes, Rock Bass, Black
Basses)
pp. 77-84

DRUM FAMILY
p. 85

SCULPIN FAMILY
pp. 86-88

TEMPERATE BASS FAMILY
(White Bass)
p. 89

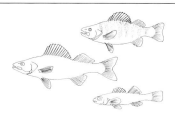

PERCH FAMILY
(Perch, Walleye, Sauger, Darter)
pp. 90-92

---

*¹ Suggested by Mervin F. Roberts in **Fisheries**, Jan./Feb. 1986, p. 66.*

EXPLANATION OF INFORMATION
IN SPECIES DESCRIPTIONS

NAMES — The common and scientific (Latinized) names of fishes (except the subspecies names for Cutthroat Trout) conform to those recommended by the American Fisheries Society. "Other names" are local names or alternate common names. They are listed so the reader can associate the recommended common names with ones that may be more familiar.

LENGTHS — Two lengths are usually given, for example: 12" (23"). The first is a typical adult size for individuals taken by sampling or sport fishing, while the second (in parentheses) is the usual Montana maximum (measured from the tip of the snout to the farthest tip of the tail fin); it is not necessarily the record length, but a length seldom exceeded. If only one length is given, it is a typical length. (Record weights for fishes taken by sport fishing are given on pp. 94-95.)

MAPS — The known distribution of a species or subspecies is shown in color (magenta) on the map. When large areas are indicated, there may be population gaps or sparse populations within the range resulting from lack of suitable streams and lakes, or from failure of the species to reach local areas through natural migration or introduction by man. On the other hand, maps for some species may not include all locations. This is especially true for maps of sport and forage fishes used in private ponds.

HABITAT — The habitat description refers to the preferred or usual habitat and is simplified for the sake of brevity.

CONSIDERATIONS IN IDENTIFYING FISHES

Location — As a rule, the place where the fish to be identified was taken should be within the known range of the species (see distribution map) and should fit the habitat described.

Color — Color alone is seldom reliable in fish identification. It may vary from one habitat to another, from season to season (many fishes are more colorful at spawning time), and between sexes. Also, color usually changes after death. Color illustrations in this book feature adult males, which are usually the most brightly colored individuals.

Body shape and hybrids — There is sometimes variation in body shape between breeding males and females and between immature fish and adults. Then, too, a hybrid (a cross between different species or subspecies) is sometimes encountered. A hybrid's characteristics are usually intermediate between those of the parental forms.

Identifying fishes is not always easy, but with practice you will become skillful.

IMAGINARY FISH
SHOWING EXTERNAL FEATURES
(no fish has all of these features)

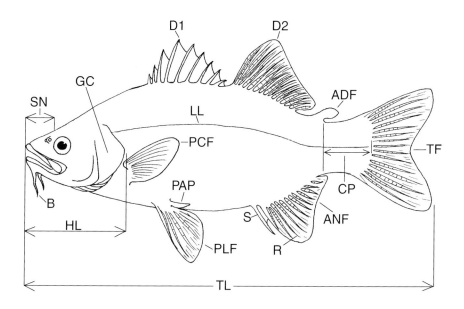

ADF — Adipose fin
ANF — Anal fin
B — Barbel
CP — Caudal peduncle
D1 — First dorsal fin (spines)
D2 — Second dorsal fin (rays)
GC — Gill cover
HL — Head length

LL — Lateral line
PAP — Pelvic axillary process
PCF — Pectoral fin
PLF — Pelvic fin
R — Ray
S — Spine
SN — Snout
TF — Tail fin or caudal fin
TL — Total length

COUNTS USED IN FISH IDENTIFICATION

HOW TO COUNT SCALES IN THE LATERAL LINE
The lateral line (shown in the illustration on p. 11) is a series of sensory pores. Scales along it (each has a pore) are counted from the gill cover to the base of the tail fin. The base is located at the crease created in the caudal peduncle when the tail is bent sideways. Scales behind the crease are not counted. When the lateral line is missing, the scales along the side where it would be are counted (referred to as lateral series).

HOW TO COUNT FIN RAYS
Rays are counted at their bases, not their tips. All rays in the pelvic and pectoral fins are counted. Rays in the dorsal and anal fins are counted as shown in the following illustration:

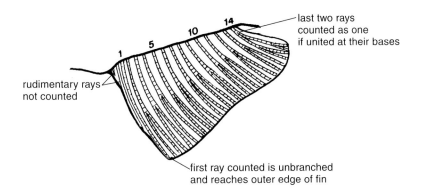

HOW TO COUNT GILL RAKERS
All gill rakers, including rudiments on the first (outermost) arch, are counted.

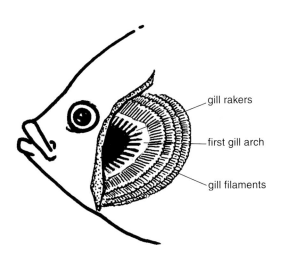

drawings by Vern Craig

GLOSSARY

(Also, see IMAGINARY FISH SHOWING EXTERNAL FEATURES and COUNTS USED IN FISH IDENTIFICATION on pp. 11-12.)

Adipose fin — A small, rayless, fleshy fin along the midline of the back behind the dorsal fin. Present on members of trout, bullhead catfish, smelt, and trout-perch families.

Anal fin — The unpaired fin along the midline of a fish's underside in front of the tail fin.

Axillary process — See *Pelvic axillary process.*

Barbel — A slender, flexible projection on the mouth or chin used for touch or taste. Barbels may be long and fleshy as in catfishes, or flaplike or threadlike as in some minnows.

Belly — The underside of a fish from just behind the pectoral fins to the front of the anal fin.

Breast — The underside of a fish from the junction of the gill covers to just behind the pectoral fins.

Canine teeth — Strong, sharp, cone-shaped teeth, longer than other teeth, as in the Walleye.

Caudal peduncle — The part of a fish's body between the anal fin and the base of the tail fin.

Char (*charr*) — See p. 96.

Cold, cool, warmwater fishes — See p. 96.

Cutthroat slash — A red to orange line in the skin fold on each side of the lower jaw of Cutthroat Trout, hence the name of this species.

Dorsal fin(s) — A fin or two fins along the midline of the back, usually midway between the head and tail fin, with supporting rays and/or spines.

Endangered species — As used in this book, a designation under the federal Endangered Species Act for a native Montana fish that is in danger of extinction throughout all or a significant portion of its range. Endangered species are indicated in the list of fishes starting on p. 98. They retain their status as state fishes of special concern.

Fish of special concern — A designation jointly made by Montana Fish, Wildlife & Parks and the Montana Chapter of the American Fisheries Society for a native fish with limited habitats and in most cases limited numbers in Montana. A fish so indicated is not necessarily threatened or endangered but may require special attention. Fishes of special concern are indicated in the list of fishes starting on p. 98.

Gill rakers — Knobby or comblike projections on the front edge of the gill arches (see illustration on p. 12). Some fishes use them to filter small food organisms from the water. Gill rakers are seen by raising the gill cover.

Gonopodium — A rodlike extension of anal fin rays in male livebearers used to transfer sperm into the female.

Lateral line — A line of pores along a fish's side (one per scale if the fish has scales) that open into an underlying sensory canal. The lateral line is said to be complete if it extends from the gill cover to the base of the tail fin, and incomplete if it extends only partway. See HOW TO COUNT SCALES IN THE LATERAL LINE on p. 12.

Length — see *Total length* below; also LENGTHS on p. 10.

Native — A species occurring naturally in a particular area (not introduced by man).

Nuptial tubercles — Small, horny structures that develop on the skin of some fishes during breeding season.

Paired fins — The pectoral and pelvic fins. They occupy somewhat the same position as the fore-limbs and hindlimbs, respectively, in higher animals.

Palatine teeth — Teeth in the roof of the mouth on a pair of bones that extend outward and rearward on each side (see illustration on p. 86).

Parr marks — Dark, vertical blotches on the young of many members of the trout family; these may persist to adulthood in a few species.

Pectoral fins — The forward or uppermost paired fins on each side just behind the head.

Pelvic axillary process — A fleshy or scaly dagger-shaped projection at the base of each pelvic fin, as in members of the trout family.

Pelvic fins — The paired fins on the lower body behind or below the pectoral fins.

Prickles — Small projections on the skin (apparently vestiges of scales) that feel rough to the touch, as in sculpins.

Rays (soft rays) — The supporting structures in fins that are segmented (crossed by grooves o striations), usually flexible, and often branched.

Rudiment or rudimentary — Not fully developed; for example, the short, unbranched rays in some fins.

Soft rayed — A fin without spines or a fish with only soft-rayed fins.

Spines — 1. Fin rays that are not branched or segmented (i.e., not crossed by grooves or striations) and that are usually sharp and stiff. 2. The hardened soft rays on such fishes as Common Carp and members of the bullhead catfish family. 3. The straight or curved, sharp structures on a bone, such as spines on the gill cover of sculpins.

Spiny-rayed fish — A fish in which the first dorsal fin or the front part of the dorsal fin has spine type rays. Usually, it also has spiny fin rays in the anal fin.

Threatened species — A designation under the federal Endangered Species Act for a native Montana fish that is likely to become an endangered species within the foreseeable future. At the time of writing, no Montana fish is designated threatened.

Total length — The straight-line distance from the tip of the snout (with mouth closed) to the farthest tip of the tail fin.

Turbid — Having sediment suspended in the water; muddy or silty.

DESCRIPTIONS OF MONTANA FISHES

STURGEON FAMILY
Acipenseridae

Sturgeons are descendants of an ancient group of fishes. They are characterized by a long snout with the mouth underneath behind four long barbels, and a "backbone" that extends into the enlarged upper lobe of the tail fin. Instead of the typical overlapping scales they have several lengthwise rows of shieldlike plates.

SHOVELNOSE STURGEON
Scaphirhynchus platorynchus

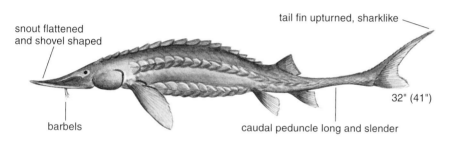

snout flattened and shovel shaped

tail fin upturned, sharklike

32" (41")

barbels

caudal peduncle long and slender

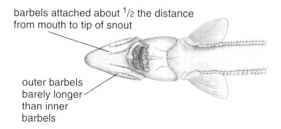

barbels attached about $1/2$ the distance from mouth to tip of snout

outer barbels barely longer than inner barbels

OTHER NAME: Hackleback.

COLOR: See p. 49.

OTHER CHARACTERISTICS: Dorsal fin has 30 to 36 rays; anal fin has 18 to 23 rays.

SIMILAR SPECIES: (1) Pallid Sturgeon differs in position and lengths of barbels, and has more rays in its dorsal and anal fins. (2) See White Sturgeon.

HABITAT: Large rivers over sand or gravel, often in strong current; also impoundments of these rivers. Tolerates turbid water.

ORIGIN: Native in Missouri-Mississippi river drainage, including Montana.

PALLID STURGEON
Scaphirhynchus albus

caudal peduncle long and slender

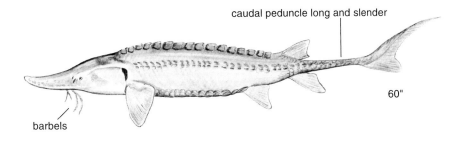

60"

barbels

barbels attached close to mouth,
about ¹/₃ the distance from mouth
to tip of snout

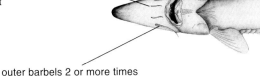

outer barbels 2 or more times
the length of inner barbels
(be alert for broken barbels)

COLOR: Back and sides gray to tan, underside yellow to white.

OTHER CHARACTERISTICS: Dorsal fin has 37 to 42 rays; anal fin has 24 to 28 rays.

SIMILAR SPECIES: See (1) Shovelnose Sturgeon and (2) White Sturgeon.

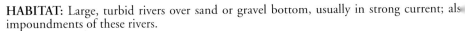

HABITAT: Large, turbid rivers over sand or gravel bottom, usually in strong current; als impoundments of these rivers.

ORIGIN: Native in Missouri-Mississippi river drainage, including Montana.

COMMENT: Rare in Montana and also rare in downstream states. Listed as endangere under the federal Endangered Species Act.

WHITE STURGEON
Acipenser transmontanus

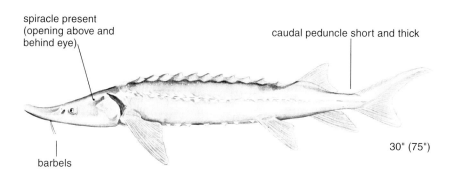

spiracle present
(opening above and
behind eye)

caudal peduncle short and thick

30" (75")

barbels

COLOR: Gray.

SIMILAR SPECIES: Other Montana sturgeons have a long, slender caudal peduncle, have no spiracle, and are found only east of the Continental Divide.

HABITAT: Landlocked White Sturgeon live in large, cool rivers and lakes.

ORIGIN: Pacific Coast, from mid-California to Alaska, where it is anadromous (spending part of its life at sea and ascending rivers to spawn). Also native, but landlocked, in upper Columbia River Drainage including Kootenai River downstream from the falls in Montana.

COMMENT: The Kootenai River White Sturgeon is listed as endangered under the federal Endangered Species Act. Montana's population decreased significantly after construction of Libby Dam in 1972 and may have vanished from the state.

PADDLEFISH FAMILY
Polyodontidae

Paddlefishes are primitive fishes, relicts of a bygone era. They are readily identified by the long paddlelike snout, long, tapered gill covers, and the "backbone" bent up into the upper lobe of the tail fin.

PADDLEFISH
Polyodon spathula

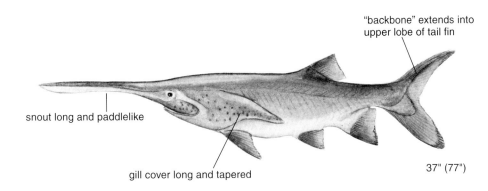

"backbone" extends into upper lobe of tail fin

snout long and paddlelike

gill cover long and tapered

37" (77")

OTHER NAME: Spoonbill Cat.

COLOR: See p. 49.

OTHER CHARACTERISTICS: Body smooth and virtually scaleless.

HABITAT: Slow or quiet waters of large rivers or impoundments. Spawns on gravel bars of large rivers during spring high water. Tolerates or perhaps seeks turbid water.

ORIGIN: Native to Montana. Year-round populations in Fort Peck Lake and in dredge cut below Fort Peck Dam. Spring spawning run from North Dakota up Missouri River into Montana. Majority of run branches off into Yellowstone River, while remainder continues up Missouri River to Fort Peck Dam. Also, spawning run from Fort Peck Lake upstream into Missouri River.

COMMENT: This is a fish of special concern as there are only six major reproducing populations left in the United States. Two of these are in Montana. It swims with its mouth open and strains plankton (microscopic plants and animals that drift or swim weakly) from the water with its comblike gill rakers. Function of the paddlelike snout is not completely understood. may be a sensory organ for locating concentrations of food, and/or even a stabilizer to prevent the nosediving that might otherwise result from the drag created by water entering the gaping mouth.

GAR FAMILY
Lepisosteidae

Like sturgeons and Paddlefish, gars are primitive fishes, little changed over millions of years. Montana's only representative, the Shortnose Gar, is a typical member of the family.

SHORTNOSE GAR
Lepisosteus platostomus

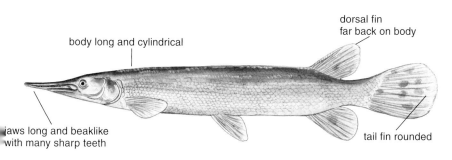

dorsal fin
far back on body

body long and cylindrical

jaws long and beaklike
with many sharp teeth

tail fin rounded

25" (29")

COLOR: Olive green to brown, grading to white below.

OTHER CHARACTERISTICS: Body covered with thick, nonoverlapping, diamond-shaped scales.

HABITAT: Large rivers, their backwaters, and impoundments.

ORIGIN: Native in Mississippi and Missouri river drainages upstream to Fort Peck Dam in Montana.

COMMENT: Rare in Montana and designated a fish of special concern. Gar eggs are poisonous to humans.

PIKE FAMILY
Esocidae

Family members have a flattened, beaklike snout and a large mouth with many sharp teeth. The dorsal fin is placed far back on the long body. The "Wall-eyed Pike" is not a true pike but a member of the perch family (p. 91).

NORTHERN PIKE
Esox lucius

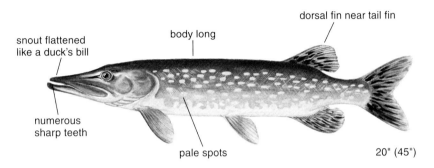

dorsal fin near tail fin

body long

snout flattened
like a duck's bill

numerous
sharp teeth

pale spots

20" (45")

OTHER NAMES: Pike, Northern, Pickerel, Jack, Hammer handle, Slimer.

COLOR: See p. 50.

SIMILAR SPECIES: The Tiger Muskellunge—a sterile hybrid of the Northern Pike and Muskellunge—has been planted in a few small reservoirs east of the Continental Divide (the Muskellunge is not present in Montana waters). The Tiger Muskellunge's body has vertical greenish stripes on a light background (juvenile Northern Pike have light vertical stripes on a dark background).

Northern Pike

HABITAT: Bays of lakes and reservoirs; pools and backwaters of streams. Seeks areas with dense vegetation.

ORIGIN: Natural distribution is circumpolar—i.e., across northern Eurasia and northern North America. Native to Montana in the South Saskatchewan River Drainage. Now widely distributed in the state due to introductions by humans.

COMMENT: The Northern Pike is a voracious fish that eats mostly other fishes. Its unauthorized introduction into waters west of the Continental Divide has destroyed several native trout populations; as this species moves down the Columbia River Drainage it poses a significant threat to native fish populations.

Tiger Muskellunge

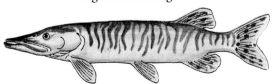

MOONEYE FAMILY
Hiodontidae

Members of this family are moderate-sized fishes with deep, flat-sided bodies covered by large, silvery scales. The dorsal fin is set back over the long anal fin. Montana has one species.

GOLDEYE
Hiodon alosoides

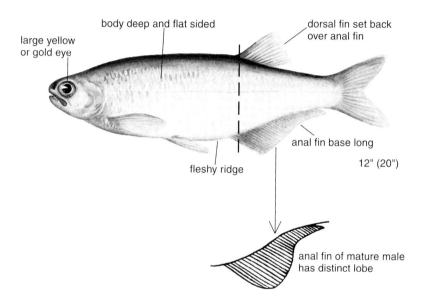

body deep and flat sided

large yellow or gold eye

dorsal fin set back over anal fin

anal fin base long

12" (20")

fleshy ridge

anal fin of mature male has distinct lobe

OTHER NAMES: Skipjack, Shiner, Shad.

COLOR: See p. 50.

OTHER CHARACTERISTICS: Large scales. Well-developed teeth on jaws, roof of mouth, and tongue.

HABITAT: Large rivers and reservoirs; adapted to turbid water.

ORIGIN: Native to Montana.

SUCKER FAMILY
Catostomidae

A typical sucker has its mouth on the underside of the head with extensible lips adapted for sucking food from the bottom. The mouth is always toothless and the fins soft rayed.

Young suckers may be confused with minnows. The former, however, usually have a "sucker mouth," never have barbels, and have the anal fin set farther back on the body. On suckers the distance from the front of the anal fin to the tip of the snout is over $2^1/2$ times the distance from the front of the anal fin to the base of the tail fin. This is also true on Common Carp and Goldfish, but they are easily told from suckers by the saw-toothed spines in their dorsal and anal fins. If the proportion is less than $2^1/2$ times, the fish is a minnow.

POSITION OF ANAL FIN
Sucker

Minnow

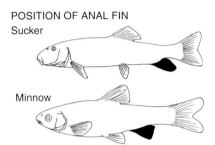

SHORTHEAD REDHORSE
Moxostoma macrolepidotum

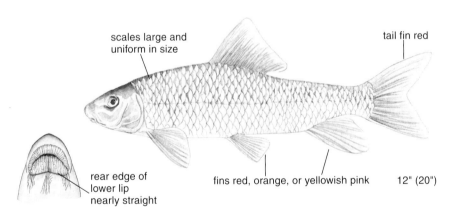

scales large and uniform in size

tail fin red

rear edge of lower lip nearly straight

fins red, orange, or yellowish pink   12" (20")

COLOR: Sides golden or silvery, back olive to brown with golden reflections, underside white to yellow. Upper body scales have dark pigment at their bases.

SIMILAR SPECIES: No other Montana sucker has a red tail fin.

HABITAT: Moderately large rivers with sand, gravel, or rocky bottom, intermediate temperatures, and swift current.

ORIGIN: Native to Montana.

LARGESCALE SUCKER
Catostomus macrocheilus

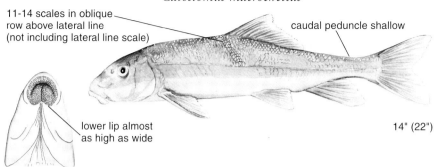

11-14 scales in oblique row above lateral line (not including lateral line scale)

caudal peduncle shallow

lower lip almost as high as wide

14" (22")

OTHER NAME: Coarsescale Sucker.

COLOR: Back and sides dark olive gray, changing abruptly to white or yellowish on underside.

OTHER CHARACTERISTICS: Dorsal fin usually has 13 to 15 rays, its base is long. Scales are medium sized, 62 to 80 in lateral line.

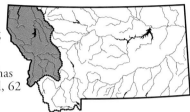

SIMILAR SPECIES: (1) White Sucker has 8 to 10 scales above lateral line, lower lip is much wider than high. It is not found west of Continental Divide (Largescale Sucker is only west of Divide). (2) See Longnose Sucker.

HABITAT: Lakes and rivers.

ORIGIN: Native to Montana.

WHITE SUCKER
Catostomus commersoni

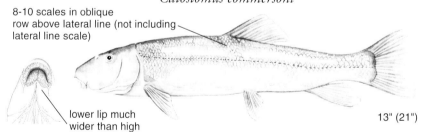

8-10 scales in oblique row above lateral line (not including lateral line scale)

lower lip much wider than high

13" (21")

OTHER NAMES: Common Sucker, Coarsescale Sucker.

COLOR: Dusky olive brown to nearly black above, shading to cream or white below.

OTHER CHARACTERISTICS: Dorsal fin has 11 to 13 rays. Scales are medium sized, 60 to 75 in lateral line.

SIMILAR SPECIES: (1) Longnose Sucker has a longer snout and smaller scales (its smaller scales make it noticeably smoother to the touch). (2) see Largescale Sucker.

HABITAT: All kinds of lakes and streams but avoids rapid current—very adaptable.

ORIGIN: Native to Montana.

LONGNOSE SUCKER
Catostomus catostomus

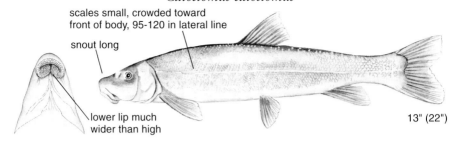

scales small, crowded toward front of body, 95-120 in lateral line

snout long

lower lip much wider than high

13" (22")

OTHER NAME: Finescale Sucker.

COLOR: Back, upper sides, and head to below the eye dark olive to slate; underparts white or yellow. Breeding males are nearly jet black on upper half of head and body and may have red midside band.

OTHER CHARACTERISTICS: Has 9 to 12 rays in dorsal fin, and more than 15 scales above lateral line (see illustration for either White Sucker or Largescale Sucker).

SIMILAR SPECIES: (1) Largescale Sucker's dorsal fin base is noticeably longer than the Longnose Sucker's; Largescale also has a shorter snout and larger scales. See (2) White Sucker and (3) Mountain Sucker.

HABITAT: Clear, cold streams and lakes; sometimes moderately warm waters and turbid waters.

ORIGIN: Native to Montana.

MOUNTAIN SUCKER
Catostomus platyrhynchus

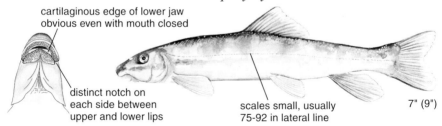

cartilaginous edge of lower jaw obvious even with mouth closed

distinct notch on each side between upper and lower lips

scales small, usually 75-92 in lateral line

7" (9")

COLOR: Back and upper sides dusky or dark green with black specks; may have dark mottling shaped like saddles across the back; lower body whitish. Both sexes have a reddish-orange band along sides during breeding season; band is brighter, longer, and wider in male.

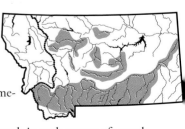

OTHER CHARACTERISTICS: Mouth is so long it sometimes exceeds head width.

SIMILAR SPECIES: No other Montana sucker has a notch in each corner of mouth.

HABITAT: Clear, cold streams with rubble, gravel, or sand bottoms; sometimes turbid streams but seldom lakes.

ORIGIN: Native to Montana.

BLUE SUCKER
Cycleptus elongatus

eye closer to back of head
than to tip of snout

dorsal fin long and
sickle shaped

lips have
wartlike bumps

caudal peduncle long

26" (32")

COLOR: Back and sides dark blue to dark olive, underside white.

HABITAT: Swift currents of medium to large rivers.

ORIGIN: Native to Montana.

COMMENT: A fish of special concern. It has been adversely affected by habitat changes, particularly those caused by large dams that block passage to spawning grounds, alter the streamflow, and eliminate peak flows that initiate spawning runs. Dams also discharge cold, clear water as opposed to the warm, turbid waters in which this species evolved.

BIGMOUTH BUFFALO
Ictiobus cyprinellus

dorsal fin long and
sickle shaped

top of mouth about level
with lower rim of eye

lips nearly smooth,
upper lip thin

29" (43")

COLOR: Usually dark colored (brownish or blackish), often with a coppery sheen; sometimes greenish or gray. Underside whitish or yellow; fins dark.

SIMILAR SPECIES: (1) Smallmouth Buffalo's color is generally lighter, top of mouth is well below lower margin of eye, and lips are thicker and more deeply grooved. See (2) River Carpsucker and (3) Common Carp.

HABITAT: Large rivers and reservoirs.

ORIGIN: Native to Montana.

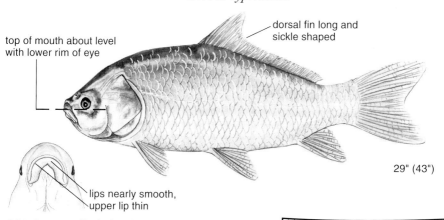

SMALLMOUTH BUFFALO
Ictiobus bubalus

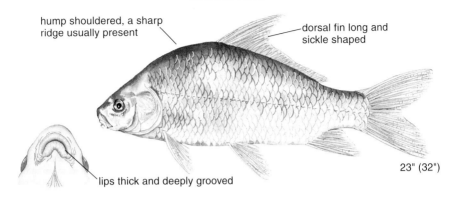

hump shouldered, a sharp ridge usually present

dorsal fin long and sickle shaped

23" (32")

lips thick and deeply grooved

COLOR: Bronze to slate or olive on back and sides, often with a bluish cast; lighter below. Fins dark.

OTHER CHARACTERISTICS: Top of upper lip is well below lower margin of eye.

SIMILAR SPECIES: See (1) Bigmouth Buffalo, (2) River Carpsucker, and (3) Common Carp.

HABITAT: Reservoirs, quiet areas of rivers, and sometimes small streams.

ORIGIN: Native to Montana.

RIVER CARPSUCKER
Carpiodes carpio

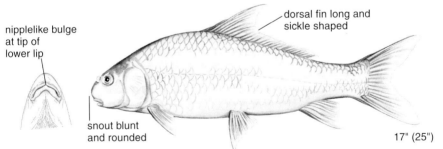

dorsal fin long and sickle shaped

nipplelike bulge at tip of lower lip

snout blunt and rounded

17" (25")

OTHER NAMES: White Carp, Silver Carp.

COLOR: Sides silvery, back brown to olive, underside white. Lower fins whitish.

SIMILAR SPECIES: (1) Buffalos are darker colored; also, they do not have a nipplelike bulge at tip of lower lip. Smallmouth Buffalo usually has a sharp ridge on back in front of dorsal fin; top of Bigmouth Buffalo's mouth is about level with lower margin of eye. (2) See Common Carp.

HABITAT: Small to large rivers, especially backwaters; also reservoirs.

ORIGIN: Native to Montana.

MINNOW FAMILY
Cyprinidae

Although the term "minnow" is often applied to all young or small fishes, it is properly used only in reference to members of the minnow family. Most minnows are small (less than 5 inches), but some become large. For example, Common Carp and Northern Squawfish reach sizes in excess of 2 feet.

Family members have a toothless mouth and soft-rayed fins (except for a spine in the dorsal and anal fins of Common Carp and Goldfish). Some have barbels.

Adult specimens of most minnows can be identified from the pictures, descriptions, and comparisons in this guide. Information in the table on p. 42 will help with look-alikes, and the distribution maps will give valuable hints.

The bulk of a typical minnow population, however, is comprised of juveniles. Some immature minnows are distinctive and identifiable, but many are so similar and have key characters (such as barbels) so hard to find that they cannot be positively identified in the field.

COMMON CARP
Cyprinus carpio

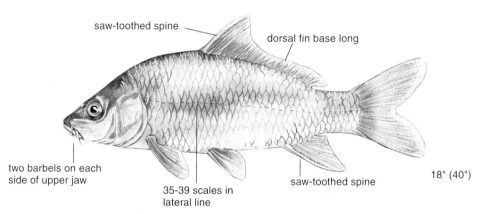

saw-toothed spine

dorsal fin base long

two barbels on each side of upper jaw

35-39 scales in lateral line

saw-toothed spine

18" (40")

COLOR: Overall bronze with a dark-brown to olive-green back and yellowish underside.

OTHER CHARACTERISTICS: Some individuals, called Mirror Carp, have enlarged scales scattered over the body with bare patches between. Leather Carp are scaleless.

SIMILAR SPECIES: Goldfish have no barbels and fewer scales in the lateral line. Common Carp and Goldfish are distinguished from suckers (especially the River Carpsucker and the buffalos) and from all other minnows by the saw-toothed spine in dorsal and anal fins; also, suckers do not have barbels.

HABITAT: Primarily lakes and reservoirs, where it seeks moderately warm water and shallows. Also rivers, where it prefers pools and backwaters. Congregates in areas of organic enrichment, such as sewage outfalls. Tolerates turbid water and low dissolved oxygen; avoids cold water and swift, rocky streams (thus, usually not found in trout streams).

ORIGIN: Native to Eurasia. Introduced into Montana.

GOLDFISH
Carassius auratus

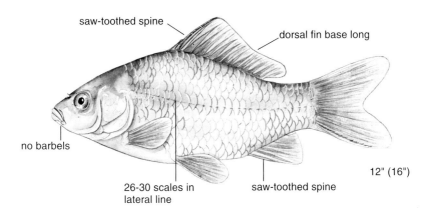

saw-toothed spine

dorsal fin base long

no barbels

26-30 scales in
lateral line

saw-toothed spine

12" (16")

COLOR: Variable. Ranges from red, orange, black, white or any combination of these in cultured varieties to dark olive brown in individuals that have reverted to the wild.

SIMILAR SPECIES: See Common Carp.

HABITAT: Lakes and ponds with weedy shallows that are somewhat warm in summer.

ORIGIN: Native to eastern Asia. Montana populations are the result of unauthorized releases of pets into state waters.

COMMENT: Goldfish can become so numerous in the wild that they crowd out more desirable species. It is illegal to release them in any lake, pond, or stream in the state.

UTAH CHUB
Gila atraria

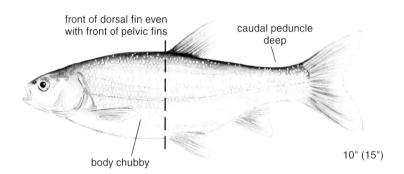

front of dorsal fin even
with front of pelvic fins

caudal peduncle
deep

body chubby

10" (15")

COLOR: Back olive brown to nearly black, occasionally bluish; sides usually brassy but sometimes silvery. Underside usually whitish or silvery.

OTHER CHARACTERISTICS: No barbels.

SIMILAR SPECIES: (1) Other Montana chubs have barbels and a shallower caudal peduncle; also, adult size is smaller. (2) An immature Fathead Minnow can be distinguished from a small Utah Chub by the former's rounded dorsal fin and dark vertical line at base of tail fin.

HABITAT: Lakes and streams. Prefers slow-moving or still water and areas with abundant aquatic vegetation.

ORIGIN: Native to waters of ancient Lake Bonneville and Snake River Drainage above Shoshone Falls. Apparently introduced into Hebgen Lake, Montana, in the early 1930s from a fisherman's bait bucket. Has since dispersed downstream.

NORTHERN SQUAWFISH
Ptychocheilus oregonensis

tail fin
deeply forked

snout long

large, toothless mouth
extends behind front of eye
(except in small fish)

12" (27")

COLOR: Back dark greenish, silvery below. Young have prominent dark spot at base of tail fin.

OTHER CHARACTERISTICS: No barbels.

SIMILAR SPECIES: (1) A Squawfish might be mistaken for a trout, but trouts have an adipose fin and teeth in the mouth. (2) Peamouth has a small mouth. (3) Flathead Chub has barbels and longer, more pointed pectoral fins; it is not found in the same drainages as Northern Squawfish.

HABITAT: Typically lakes, but also slower currents of rivers and streams.

ORIGIN: Native to Montana.

PEAMOUTH
Mylocheilus caurinus

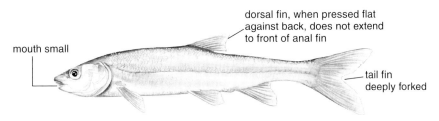

dorsal fin, when pressed flat
against back, does not extend
to front of anal fin

mouth small

tail fin
deeply forked

8" (14")

COLOR: Dark on back and silvery below; two dusky stripes along side; reddish at corners of mouth. Breeding fish have red midside stripe.

OTHER CHARACTERISTICS: Small barbel at each corner of mouth.

SIMILAR SPECIES: (1) See Northern Squawfish. (2) Adult Lake Chub is only half the size of adult Peamouth, and dorsal fin when pressed flat extends over anal fin; also, it is not found in the same drainages as Peamouth.

HABITAT: Lakes and streams, particularly weedy areas.

ORIGIN: Native to Montana.

REDSIDE SHINER
Richardsonius balteatus

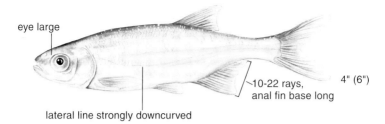

eye large

10-22 rays,
anal fin base long

4" (6")

lateral line strongly downcurved

COLOR: Dark olive to brown on back; dark midside band from snout to tail fin with a narrow light stripe above it; lower sides silver with a reddish wash; underside silvery. Breeding fish highly colored; male has brilliant red and yellow on sides and belly, female is less striking.

OTHER CHARACTERISTICS: Body moderately deep and flat sided, front of dorsal fin well behind front of pelvic fins.

SIMILAR SPECIES: Golden Shiner has a ridge on belly and golden coloration. In addition, range of the Golden is east of the Continental Divide, while the Redside's is almost exclusively west of the Divide.

HABITAT: Lakes, ponds, and rivers.

ORIGIN: Native to Montana.

GOLDEN SHINER
Notemigonus crysoleucas

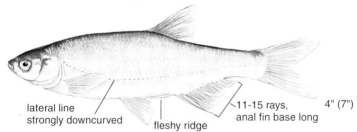

lateral line
strongly downcurved

fleshy ridge

11-15 rays,
anal fin base long

4" (7")

COLOR: Adults golden; color fades rapidly when removed from water. Young silvery with dusky midside band.

OTHER CHARACTERISTICS: Body deep and flat-sided, front of dorsal fin well behind front of pelvic fins. Head small and triangular.

SIMILAR SPECIES: See Redside Shiner.

HABITAT: Weedy ponds, lakes, and slow-moving streams.

ORIGIN: Native to eastern North America as far west as the Dakotas and Texas, and from southern Canada to the Gulf States. Almost certainly introduced into Montana.

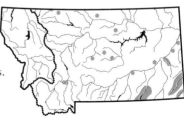

NORTHERN REDBELLY DACE
Phoxinus eos

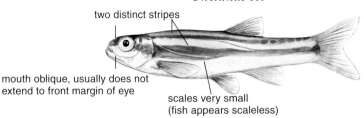

two distinct stripes

mouth oblique, usually does not
extend to front margin of eye

scales very small
(fish appears scaleless)

2" (2¹/₂")

COLOR: Olive to dark brown above; lower side and belly yellow or silvery except on adult males during summer when lower side is red. Side has two dark stripes with a light band between them; the upper stripe often breaks into spots toward tail. The lower stripe is broader and extends from snout to base of tail fin where it may end in a spot. These two lateral stripes are sometimes connected by a dark, oblique line or crossband.

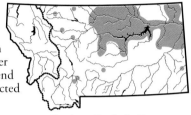

Northern Redbelly Dace

OTHER CHARACTERISTICS: Eye large. Body almost round in cross section. Front of dorsal fin behind front of pelvic fins. Lateral line incomplete and not distinct. No barbels.

SIMILAR SPECIES: (1) The hybrid of the Northern Redbelly Dace and Finescale Dace has been found at 13 locations in the Missouri River Drainage. It is usually larger than the Northern Redbelly Dace and has a larger mouth. Its midside stripe is less distinct, and its upper stripe is faint and usually broken. In practice, however, there is no sure, simple field technique for telling the hybrid from the Northern Redbelly Dace. (2) The Northern Redbelly Dace is distinguished from other small minnows by its two distinct stripes, one on midside and one on upper side, and smaller scales (see table on p. 42).

HABITAT: Clear, slow-flowing creeks, ponds, and lakes with aquatic vegetation, including filamentous algae.

ORIGIN: Native to Montana.

COMMENT: Although the Northern Redbelly Dace is fairly common in Montana, the Finescale Dace has never been recorded for the state. The hybrid persists due to a unique reproductive strategy. Typically, hybrid females breed with Redbelly Dace males, but the male's genetic material is not incorporated during egg development and is not passed on to the next generation. The offspring are all female and clones of the mother (that is, they are genetically identical to the mother). Unisexuality is not common among vertebrates but has been found in amphibians and reptiles as well as in fishes. Due to its unusual form of genetic reproduction and rarity, the Northern Redbelly Dace x Finescale Dace hybrid is a fish of special concern in Montana.

Hybrid of Northern Redbelly Dace
and Finescale Dace

upper stripe broken and faint

midside stripe dusky

mouth moderately oblique, usually
extends at least to front margin of eye

scales very small

PEARL DACE
Margariscus margarita

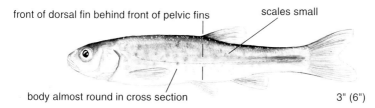

front of dorsal fin behind front of pelvic fins

scales small

body almost round in cross section

3" (6")

COLOR: Back dark, sides dusky silver, underside white; scattered dark scales give some individuals a speckled appearance. Young have a dusky midline band that fades on large specimens but may be distinct on caudal peduncle. Breeding males are orange red on the sides and below.

OTHER CHARACTERISTICS: A small, flaplike barbel is present in groove of upper lip just above each corner of mouth, sometimes absent from one or both sides. Lateral line usually complete.

SIMILAR SPECIES: (1) Although the Pearl Dace is easily confused with the Lake Chub, they can be distinguished by their barbels. The Pearl Dace has a small, flat barbel in groove of upper lip, noticeably above corner of mouth; the Lake Chub has a well-developed, rounded barbel, essentially at corner of mouth. (2) See Creek Chub.

HABITAT: Small, cool streams; some large rivers and lakes.

ORIGIN: Native to Montana.

COMMENT: Found in few Montana waters; therefore, a fish of special concern.

LAKE CHUB
Couesius plumbeus

body almost round in cross section

4" (6")

barbel (see text)

COLOR: Silver gray overall, dusky on back, underside whitish. A midside band is present but often indistinct. Scattered dark scales may be present, giving a speckled appearance. Breeding males develop reddish patches, particularly on the pectoral fin bases.

OTHER CHARACTERISTICS: A well-developed, rounded barbel is located slightly above each corner of the mouth.

SIMILAR SPECIES: See (1) Creek Chub, (2) Pearl Dace, and (3) Peamouth.

HABITAT: Mostly small streams at lower elevations; to a lesser extent, larger streams and lakes.

ORIGIN: Native to Montana.

CREEK CHUB
Semotilus atromaculatus

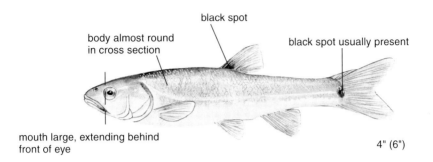

black spot

body almost round
in cross section

black spot usually present

mouth large, extending behind
front of eye

4" (6")

OTHER NAME: Horned Dace.

COLOR: Overall silvery, often with purple iridescence; back olive; underside white. Young have a prominent dark midside band extending from tip of snout to tail fin; band fades on older fish. Black spot at front of dorsal fin base may be vague in immature specimens. Breeding males usually have a reddish cast.

OTHER CHARACTERISTICS: A small, flaplike barbel is located in groove of upper lip just above each corner of mouth, sometimes absent. Breeding males have a few pronounced nuptial tubercles (horny projections) on head and smaller ones on body and pectoral fins.

SIMILAR SPECIES: No other Montana minnow has a distinct black spot on dorsal fin. (1) Pearl Dace has a smaller mouth. (2) Lake Chub has a smaller mouth and a rounded barbel. (3) A female or immature Fathead Minnow may suggest a small Creek Chub but has a smaller mouth and a dark vertical line at base of tail fin. (4) See Spottail Shiner.

HABITAT: Typically creeks. Less common in rivers and shallows of lakes.

ORIGIN: Native to Montana.

FLATHEAD CHUB
Platygobio gracilis

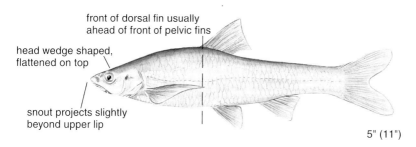

front of dorsal fin usually
ahead of front of pelvic fins

head wedge shaped,
flattened on top

snout projects slightly
beyond upper lip

5" (11")

COLOR: Very silvery, shading to brown or dusky on back.

OTHER CHARACTERISTICS: Mouth large with a conspicuous barbel at each corner. Pectoral fin sickle shaped with a long, sharply pointed tip that may extend almost to front of pelvic fin.

SIMILAR SPECIES: See (1) Sicklefin Chub, (2) Sturgeon Chub, and (3) Northern Squawfish.

HABITAT: Mostly turbid rivers and streams.

ORIGIN: Native to Montana.

SICKLEFIN CHUB
Macrhybopsis meeki

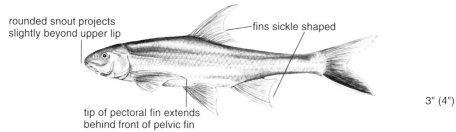

rounded snout projects
slightly beyond upper lip

fins sickle shaped

3" (4")

tip of pectoral fin extends
behind front of pelvic fin

COLOR: Light brown on back and upper sides; silvery white below.

OTHER CHARACTERISTICS: Conspicuous barbel at each corner of mouth.

SIMILAR SPECIES: (1) Could be mistaken for a small Flathead Chub. Flathead can be told by wedge-shaped head profile and pointed snout; tip of its pectoral fin does not extend behind front of pelvic fin. (2) Sturgeon Chub has keeled scales above lateral line, and its snout projects well beyond upper lip.

HABITAT: Strong currents of large turbid rivers over sand or gravel bottom.

ORIGIN: Native to Montana.

COMMENT: A fish of special concern due to its limited distribution in the state.

STURGEON CHUB
Macrhybopsis gelida

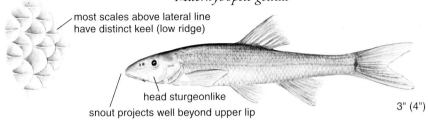

most scales above lateral line have distinct keel (low ridge)

head sturgeonlike
snout projects well beyond upper lip

3" (4")

COLOR: Back brownish, sides and underparts silvery to white.

OTHER CHARACTERISTICS: Conspicuous barbel at each corner of mouth.

SIMILAR SPECIES: (1) Could be mistaken for a small Flathead Chub but can be recognized by its smaller, horizontal mouth overhung by the snout and keeled scales above lateral line. See (2) Sicklefin Chub, and (3) Longnose Dace.

HABITAT: Currents of turbid rivers over sand, gravel, or cobble.

ORIGIN: Native to Montana.

COMMENT: Uncommon in Montana; therefore, a fish of special concern.

LONGNOSE DACE
Rhinichthys cataractae

head wedge shaped

snout projects
well beyond upper lip

3" (6")

COLOR: Back olive to black, shading to white or yellow underneath. Sides may have dark blotches. Breeding males have reddish orange on head and fins. Juveniles have a black midside stripe starting at the tip of the snout and ending at the base of the tail fin. Adults often have a dark stripe ahead of eye.

OTHER CHARACTERISTICS: Small barbel at each corner of mouth.

SIMILAR SPECIES: (1) Could be confused with small suckers, from which it is distinguished by having barbels and by the more forward placement of anal fin (see text and illustrations on p. 22). (2) Sturgeon Chub has silvery color, conspicuous barbel, and larger scales, many of which have keels.

HABITAT: Riffle areas of streams and rivers; to a lesser extent, lakes.

ORIGIN: Native to Montana.

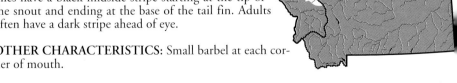

FATHEAD MINNOW
Pimephales promelas

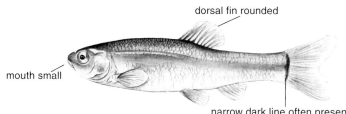

dorsal fin rounded

mouth small

2" (3")

ADULT OTHER THAN BREEDING MALE

narrow dark line often present
at base of tail fin

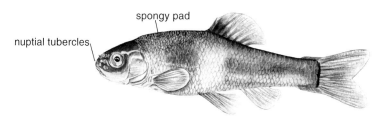

spongy pad

nuptial tubercles

BREEDING MALE

2" (3")

COLOR: Back dark olive or brown, sides dusky, pale below. Young are lighter and have a dark midside band. Breeding males nearly black with two light blotches.

OTHER CHARACTERISTICS: Body of adult is stout. Lateral line usually incomplete. Scales ahead of dorsal fin are small and crowded. First ray of dorsal fin is short, thick, and blunt—not easily seen on females and young.

SIMILAR SPECIES: Immature Fathead Minnows may be confused with small individuals of other minnow species. A narrow, dark, vertical line at base of tail fin is a clue that a minnow is a Fathead; however, other Montana minnows sometimes have a faint line at base of tail fin. See (1) Sand Shiner, (2) Brassy Minnow, (3) Creek Chub, and (4) Utah Chub.

HABITAT: Ponds, shallow lakes, slow-flowing streams. Tolerates turbid water, high temperatures, and low dissolved oxygen.

ORIGIN: Native to Montana.

BRASSY MINNOW
Hybognathus hankinsoni

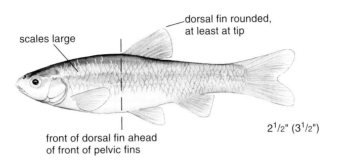

scales large

dorsal fin rounded,
at least at tip

front of dorsal fin ahead
of front of pelvic fins

2$^{1}/_{2}$" (3$^{1}/_{2}$")

COLOR: Back olive green to brown, sides yellowish or dull silver becoming brassy in adult, underside white. Dusky midside stripe usually present.

SIMILAR SPECIES: (1) Plains and Western Silvery minnows are very silvery (Brassy Minnow is usually brassy or yellow), and the dorsal fin is not rounded. (2) Fathead minnow has a drabber color, smaller scales, and an incomplete lateral line. (3) Sand Shiner has paired spots on each lateral line scale.

HABITAT: Small to medium-sized prairie streams with clear to slightly turbid water and some vegetation, often found over sand and gravel bottom. Occasionally lakes.

ORIGIN: Native to Montana.

WESTERN SILVERY MINNOW   and   PLAINS MINNOW
Hybognathus argyritis   *Hybognathus placitus*

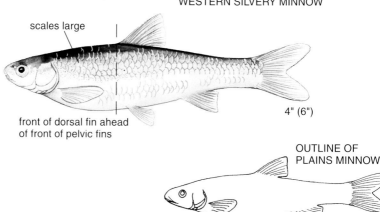

WESTERN SILVERY MINNOW

scales large

front of dorsal fin ahead
of front of pelvic fins

4" (6")

OUTLINE OF
PLAINS MINNOW

Because they are very similar, the Plains Minnow and Western Silvery Minnow are treated together. The Plains is more streamlined than the Western Silvery (see illustrations above). Also, the Plains has 15 to 22 scales across the belly from lateral line to lateral line, compared with the Western Silvery's 11 to 17. Nevertheless, there is no sure method for telling live specimens apart. Dead specimens can be identified by inspecting a bone at the base of the skull and the muscles attached to it. These features are clearly illustrated in William L. Pflieger, *The Fishes of Missouri*, Missouri Dept. of Conserv., 1975, pp. 107-108; or 1991 revision, pp. 107-108.

Montana distribution of
Western Silvery Minnow
and Plains Minnow

COLOR: Overall very silvery; back dusky or yellowish olive, underside white.

SIMILAR SPECIES: (1) Sand Shiner has paired dashes on each lateral line scale. See (2) Brassy Minnow and (3) Emerald Shiner.

HABITAT: Slower portions of medium-sized to large streams. Sometimes found in creeks and impoundments.

ORIGIN: Both species are native to Montana.

EMERALD SHINER
Notropis atherinoides

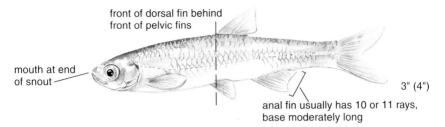

front of dorsal fin behind
front of pelvic fins

mouth at end
of snout

3" (4")

anal fin usually has 10 or 11 rays,
base moderately long

COLOR: Overall silvery with iridescent light-green back. Usually has an emerald green or silvery midside stripe, particularly toward the rear. Young are somewhat translucent.

OTHER CHARACTERISTICS: Eye large. Body slender and flat sided, fragile looking. Scales easily rubbed off.

SIMILAR SPECIES: In Brassy, Plains, and Western Silvery minnows, front of dorsal fin is ahead of front of pelvic fins, and snout slightly overhangs mouth.

HABITAT: Open water of large streams, reservoirs, and lakes.

ORIGIN: Native to Montana.

SPOTTAIL SHINER
Notropis hudsonius

front of dorsal fin even
with or slightly ahead of
front of pelvic fin

prominent black spot
(faint on older fish)

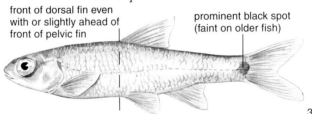

3" (5")

COLOR: Overall silvery with pale-green to olive back. Lower edge of tail fin may be whitish.

OTHER CHARACTERISTICS: Eye large, body flat sided.

SIMILAR SPECIES: The Creek Chub, like the Spottail Shiner, has a spot at base of tail fin but also has one at front of dorsal fin base. It almost always has barbels (the Spottail has none). The Creek Chub is a larger minnow but individuals that are Spottail Shiner sized have a dark midside band which may extend to tip of snout.

HABITAT: Large, clear rivers and lakes over firm bottom of sand, gravel, and rubble where vegetation is scanty or lacking. Avoids strong currents.

ORIGIN: Native range extends across much of Canada, dipping into central United States and down Eastern Seaboard. Introduced into Montana as forage for game fishes starting in 1982.

SAND SHINER
Notropis stramineus

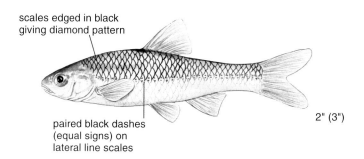

scales edged in black
giving diamond pattern

paired black dashes
(equal signs) on
lateral line scales

2" (3")

COLOR: Back light olive, sides silvery (sometimes with bluish-purple sheen), underside white. A thin black stripe along midline of back expands into a wedge at front of dorsal fin. Black dashes on lateral line scales may be faint on fish from turbid water.

OTHER CHARACTERISTICS: Eye large. Body somewhat flat sided but not deep.

SIMILAR SPECIES: Paired dashes on lateral line scales distinguish Sand Shiner from other Montana minnows.

HABITAT: Mainly streams with sand or gravel bottoms; also sandy shallows of lakes.

ORIGIN: Native to Montana.

MINNOW LATERAL LINE SCALE COUNTS
AND BARBEL CHARACTERISTICS

Species	Lateral line scale count[1]	Barbels
Goldfish	26-30	None.
Brassy Minnow	32-39	None.
Sand Shiner	32-39	None.
Plains Minnow	33-41	None.
Western Silvery Minnow	34-41	None.
Common Carp	35-39	Two on each side of upper jaw, conspicuous.
Emerald Shiner	35-41	None.
Spottail Shiner	36-42	None.
Sturgeon Chub	37-46	One at each corner of mouth, conspicuous.
Fathead Minnow	40-50[2]	None.
Flathead Chub	42-59	One at each corner of mouth, conspicuous.
Golden Shiner	44-54	None.
Sicklefin Chub	45-50	One at each corner of mouth, conspicuous.
Utah Chub	45-65	None.
Creek Chub	52-64	One in upper lip groove just ahead of each corner of mouth, small and flaplike. Sometimes absent.
Redside Shiner	52-67	None.
Lake Chub	54-70	One slightly above each corner of mouth, rounded, well developed.
Longnose Dace	58-73	One at each corner of mouth, small.
Pearl Dace	61-78	Same as Creek Chub (above). Sometimes absent from one or both sides.
Northern Squawfish	68-77	None.
Peamouth	68-79	One at each corner of mouth, small.
Northern Redbelly Dace	75-90[2]	None.

[1] When identifying minnows a quick approximate count of the lateral line scales will often narrow the field of candidates. For counting procedure see "HOW TO COUNT SCALES IN THE LATERAL LINE" on pg. 12.

[2] Scales should be counted along midside, as lateral line is incomplete.

MUDMINNOW FAMILY
Umbridae

Mudminnows are small, robust fishes with soft-rayed fins. The dorsal fin is set well back toward the tail, and the tail fin is rounded. The one Montana species has a black bar at the base of the tail fin.

CENTRAL MUDMINNOW
Umbra limi

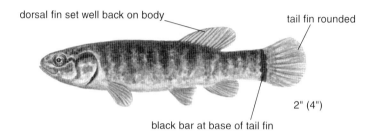

dorsal fin set well back on body

tail fin rounded

2" (4")

black bar at base of tail fin

COLOR: Overall dark colored; olive brown to brown black above, sides mottled with dark brown or may have as many as 14 irregular dark vertical bars. Underside white to yellowish.

OTHER CHARACTERISTICS: Head broad, lateral line absent. Male's anal fin long, almost reaches base of tail fin; female's anal fin does not reach base of tail fin.

SIMILAR SPECIES: (1) Plains Killifish is lighter colored and mouth is tilted upward. (2) Montana members of the livebearer family do not have a black bar at base of tail fin. (3) In members of minnow family dorsal fin is located farther forward on body.

HABITAT: Small ponds, slow-moving streams, and marshes. Usually associated with vegetation, organic debris, and mud.

ORIGIN: Unauthorized introductions into Montana. Native to central North America west of Appalachian Mountains to the Dakotas, and from southern Canada to northern Arkansas.

COMMENT: Very hardy. Can withstand water temperature extremes and comparatively high acidity. When oxygen in water insufficient, can gulp air at surface and use atmospheric oxygen. Therefore, tolerates stagnant conditions. First Montana record was in 1990 from Blacktail Creek within the Butte city limits.

KILLIFISH FAMILY
Cyprinodontidae

Killifishes are small fishes with an upturned mouth, a projecting lower lip adapted for surface feeding, and a slightly rounded or squarish tail fin. The one Montana species is boldly marked with vertical bars.

PLAINS KILLIFISH
Fundulus zebrinus

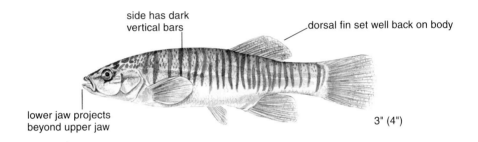

side has dark vertical bars

dorsal fin set well back on body

lower jaw projects beyond upper jaw

3" (4")

COLOR: Olive brown on back, fading to pale yellow or white below. Side has 12 to 28 dark vertical bars (bars on female are narrower and more numerous, as in illustration above).

OTHER CHARACTERISTICS: Head broad and flat, lateral line absent.

SIMILAR SPECIES: Montana members of (1) livebearer family and (2) minnow family do not have vertical bars on sides. (3) See Central Mudminnow.

HABITAT: Shallow streams with sand or gravel bottom, comparatively high alkalinity or salinity, and few other fishes.

ORIGIN: Not native to Montana. Natural range is from Platte River Drainage of Nebraska, Wyoming, and Colorado southward to Brazos and Colorado rivers in Texas and Pecos River in New Mexico and Texas. Apparently was introduced into the Big Horn River in Wyoming, moved downstream into Montana, dispersed through the lower Yellowstone River Drainage, and was spread further by bait buckets.

LIVEBEARER FAMILY
Poeciliidae

These are small fishes with mouth upturned for surface feeding. The lateral line is absent. The male's anal fin is placed forward and modified into a gonopodium, a slender structure for transferring sperm to the female. The eggs hatch internally and young emerge as free-swimming individuals.

WESTERN MOSQUITOFISH
Gambusia affinis

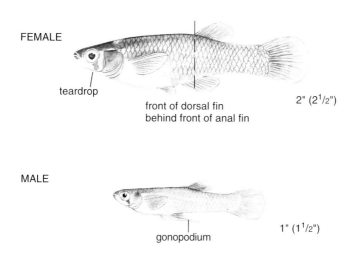

FEMALE

teardrop

front of dorsal fin
behind front of anal fin

2" (2¹/₂")

MALE

gonopodium

1" (1¹/₂")

COLOR: Light olive to dull silver.

SIMILAR SPECIES: Other livebearers in Montana waters are more colorful and do not have teardrop marking; also, dorsal fin is not placed as far back on body (on female front of dorsal fin is ahead of front of anal fin).

DISTRIBUTION AND HABITAT: Widely stocked in shallow waters across the state each year for mosquito control. Avidly eats mosquito larvae which live just below water surface. Can survive winter only in ponds or runs from thermal springs.

ORIGIN: Not native to Montana. Occurs naturally from southern Illinois and Indiana southward to the Gulf States and Mexico. Also along the Atlantic Coast from New Jersey to Florida.

TROPICAL AQUARIUM FISHES

The following livebearers are illegally released pet fishes and their progeny. None is native to Montana. Their native ranges are in southeastern United States, Mexico, and Central America. All are small—none found was larger than 3¹/2 inches. As of this writing four species are known to be established in a few warm spring streams and ponds in the western third of the state. Many, males in particular, can be identified using the pictures and color descriptions below. Females of the different species are often difficult to tell apart. Their association with males will give clues. Crossbreeding has created new varieties and color combinations that further confuse identification.

SAILFIN MOLLY
Poecilia latipinna

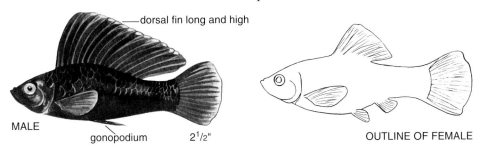

COLOR: Two varieties. Black variety (shown in illustration) is solid black. Green variety has olive back shading to silvery sides with six to eight rows of black dots and white underside.

COMMENT: Only the black variety has been verified for Montana waters. Specimens were taken from a warm spring at Beaverhead Rock in Madison County.

SHORTFIN MOLLY
Poecilia mexicana

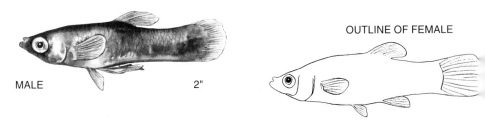

COLOR: Specimens from Montana waters have been nearly all black or heavily blotched with black on body and fins. Some have orange on tail fin.

VARIABLE PLATYFISH
Xiphophorus variatus

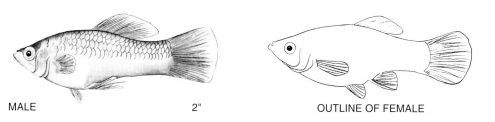

MALE   2"   OUTLINE OF FEMALE

COLOR: Variable. However, a livebearer in Montana waters with an orange-red tail fin and a golden dorsal fin is almost certain to be a Variable Platyfish. The body is typically moss green.

COMMENT: Hybrids are common where this species occurs with the Green Swordtail. Male hybrids have a short sword.

GREEN SWORDTAIL
Xiphophorus helleri

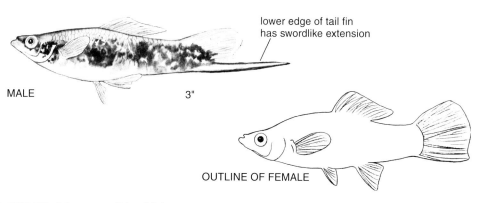

lower edge of tail fin
has swordlike extension

MALE   3"

OUTLINE OF FEMALE

COLOR: Most are solid reddish orange, some are reddish orange with black fins or reddish orange with black mottling. Swordlike tail fin usually has black edges. The classical green variety with red and yellow stripes on sides is rare in Montana waters.

SMELT FAMILY
Osmeridae

Smelts are small, slender, silvery fishes with an adipose fin and no pelvic axillary process. There is only one species in Montana.

RAINBOW SMELT
Osmerus mordax

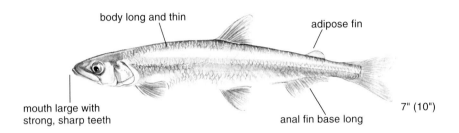

body long and thin

adipose fin

mouth large with strong, sharp teeth

anal fin base long

7" (10")

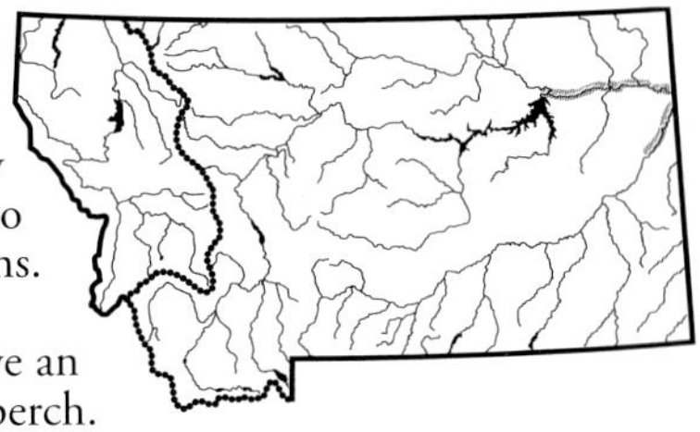

COLOR: Silvery with pink and purple iridescence, greenish on back.

OTHER CHARACTERISTICS: Scales thin and easily rubbed off. Spawning males feel like sandpaper due to numerous small nuptial tubercles on head, body, and fins.

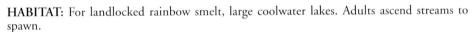

SIMILAR SPECIES: (1) Members of trout family have an axillary process at base of each pelvic fin. (2) See Trout-perch.

HABITAT: For landlocked rainbow smelt, large coolwater lakes. Adults ascend streams to spawn.

ORIGIN: Original range is off Atlantic Coast with adults ascending streams to spawn. Naturally landlocked in many inland waters in northeastern North America. Has come upstream into Montana from Lake Sakakawea (created by Garrison Dam) in North Dakota, where it was introduced.

COMMENT: Smelt have a strong fishy odor. This may account for their name.

COLOR ILLUSTRATIONS
OF GAME AND SPORT FISHES

The first length given is a typical adult size for the species; the second (in parentheses) is the usual Montana maximum length.

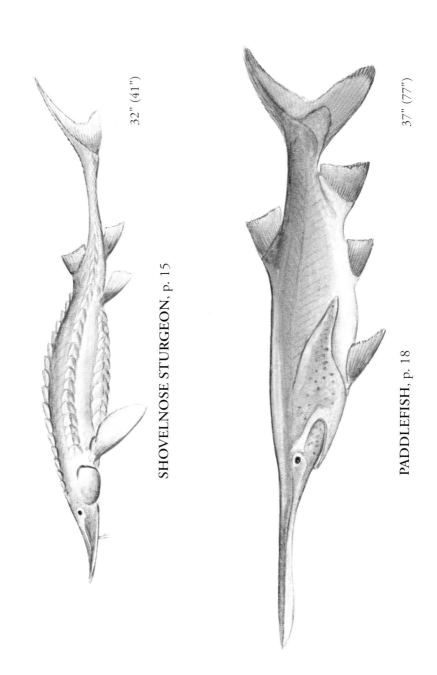

32" (41")

SHOVELNOSE STURGEON, p. 15

37" (77")

PADDLEFISH, p. 18

NORTHERN PIKE, p. 20

20" (45")

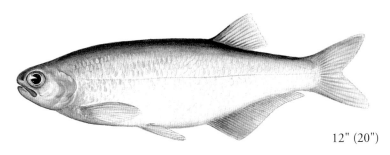

12" (20")

GOLDEYE, p. 21

24" (38")

CHINOOK SALMON, p. 58

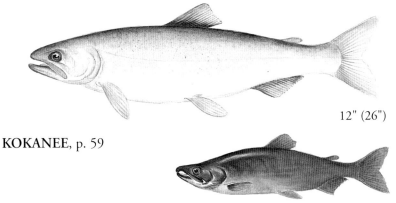

12" (26")

KOKANEE, p. 59

breeding male

12" (35")

RAINBOW TROUT, p. 60

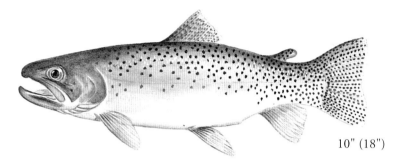

10" (18")

WESTSLOPE CUTTHROAT TROUT, p. 61

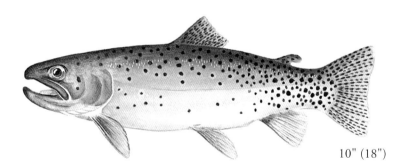

10" (18")

YELLOWSTONE CUTTHROAT TROUT, p. 62

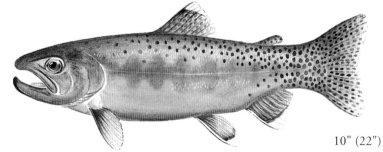

10" (22")

GOLDEN TROUT, p. 63

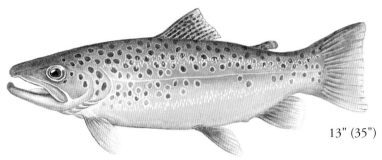

BROWN TROUT, p. 64

13" (35")

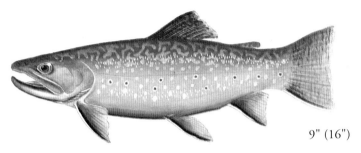

BROOK TROUT, p. 65

9" (16")

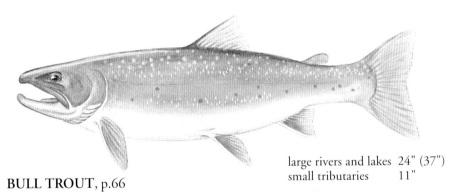

BULL TROUT, p.66

large rivers and lakes 24" (37")
small tributaries 11"

LAKE TROUT, p. 67

22" (47")

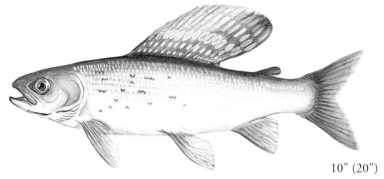

10" (20")

ARCTIC GRAYLING, p. 68

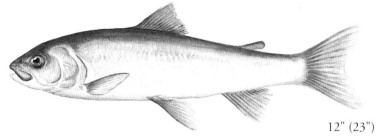

12" (23")

MOUNTAIN WHITEFISH, p. 69

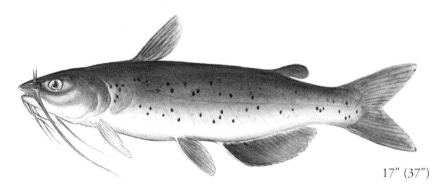

17" (37")

CHANNEL CATFISH, p. 73

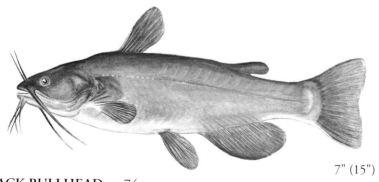

7" (15")

BLACK BULLHEAD, p. 74

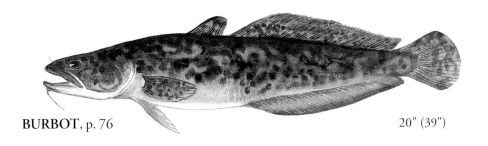

BURBOT, p. 76 20" (39")

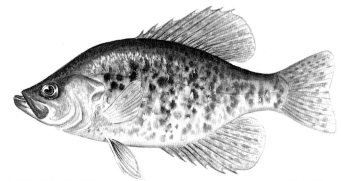

BLACK CRAPPIE, p. 77 9" (16")

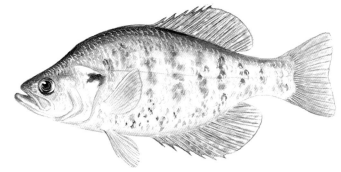

WHITE CRAPPIE, p. 78 9" (16")

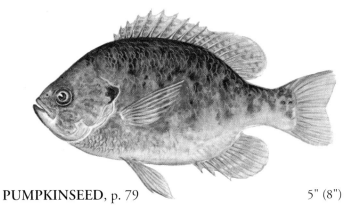

PUMPKINSEED, p. 79 5" (8")

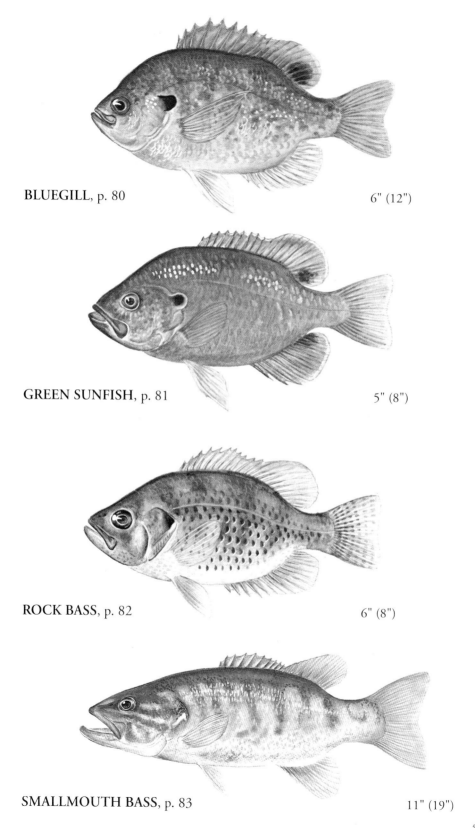

BLUEGILL, p. 80   6" (12")

GREEN SUNFISH, p. 81   5" (8")

ROCK BASS, p. 82   6" (8")

SMALLMOUTH BASS, p. 83   11" (19")

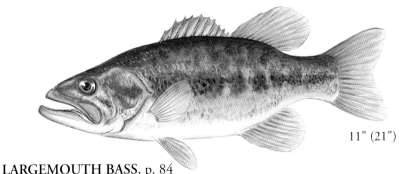

11" (21")

LARGEMOUTH BASS, p. 84

8" (15")

YELLOW PERCH, p. 90

16" (33")

WALLEYE, p. 91

SAUGER, p. 91

13" (28")

TROUT FAMILY
Salmonidae

Montana members of this family are Pacific salmons, trouts (including chars), whitefishes, and Arctic Grayling. All have an adipose fin and pelvic axillary processes; the young of most species have parr marks. Colors may vary with habitat, season, and sex.

COMPARISON OF ARCTIC GRAYLING, WHITEFISHES, PACIFIC SALMONS, TROUTS, AND CHARS

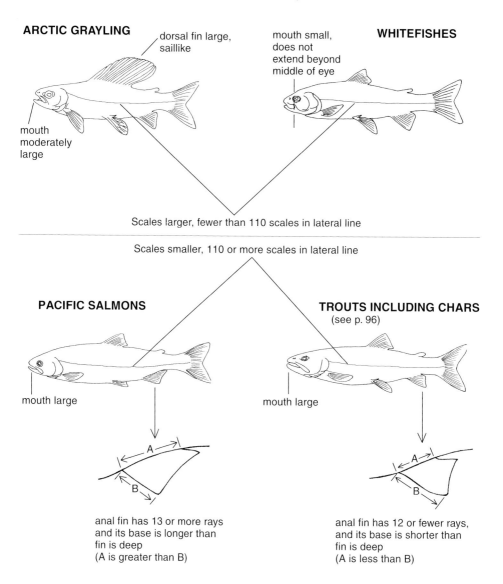

ARCTIC GRAYLING

dorsal fin large, saillike

mouth moderately large

mouth small, does not extend beyond middle of eye

WHITEFISHES

Scales larger, fewer than 110 scales in lateral line

Scales smaller, 110 or more scales in lateral line

PACIFIC SALMONS

mouth large

TROUTS INCLUDING CHARS
(see p. 96)

mouth large

anal fin has 13 or more rays and its base is longer than fin is deep
(A is greater than B)

anal fin has 12 or fewer rays, and its base is shorter than fin is deep
(A is less than B)

57

CHINOOK SALMON
Oncorhynchus tshawytscha

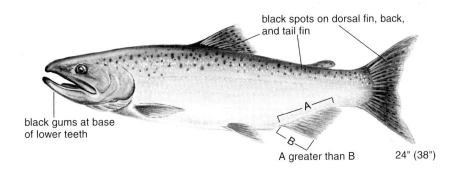

black spots on dorsal fin, back, and tail fin

black gums at base of lower teeth

A greater than B   24" (38")

OTHER NAME: King Salmon.

COLOR: See p. 50.

OTHER CHARACTERISTICS: Anal fin usually has 14 to 19 rays; its base is longer than base of dorsal fin. Has 26 or fewer gill rakers on first arch. Breeding males develop an elongated, hooked snout and enlarged teeth. Females change little. Breeding fish of both sexes darken in color, males more than females.

SIMILAR SPECIES: (1) Trouts have 12 or fewer rays in anal fin (it is deeper than long). (2) See Kokanee.

HABITAT: Landlocked Chinook Salmon live in large, deep lakes and spawn in tributary streams. The young may stay in the stream for a year or two before migrating downstream to the lake. There are no reproducing populations in Montana.

ORIGIN: Introduced into Montana. Natural range is Pacific Ocean and its tributaries. Adults ascend streams of western North America and northeastern Asia to spawn.

COMMENT: In recent years Chinook Salmon, bred to spend their entire lives in freshwater, have been stocked in Fort Peck Lake.

KOKANEE
Oncorhynchus nerka

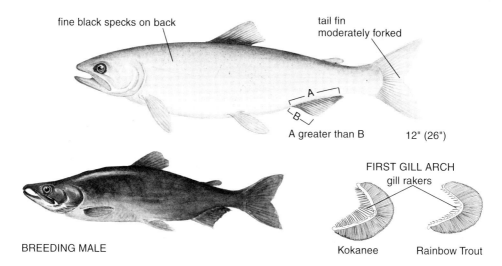

fine black specks on back

tail fin moderately forked

A

B

A greater than B

12" (26")

FIRST GILL ARCH
gill rakers

Kokanee   Rainbow Trout

BREEDING MALE

OTHER NAMES: Kokanee Salmon, Blueback, Silver.

The lower fish is a breeding male. When younger he looked like the upper fish. In maturing he had a striking color change and he developed an elongated, hooked snout, enlarged teeth, a small hump behind the head, and embedded scales. A breeding female changes less dramatically. Her color ranges from dark gray with dark-green back to dull red with dark red on the back.

COLOR: See p. 50.

OTHER CHARACTERISTICS: Anal fin has 13 to 17 rays; its base is longer than base of dorsal fin. Has 29 to 40 gill rakers on first arch.

SIMILAR SPECIES: (1) Silver-colored Rainbow Trout are often miscalled Kokanee. The anal fin base of Rainbow and other trouts is shorter than the fin is deep; the Kokanee's anal fin base is longer than the fin is deep (see illustrations at bottom of p. 57). Trouts have 26 or fewer gill rakers on first arch; the Kokanee has 29 or more and these are longer, thinner, and more crowded (see illustrations above). (2) Chinook Salmon has black spots on back, dorsal fin, and tail fin, and 26 or fewer gill rakers on first arch (these are stouter and more widely spaced than the Kokanee's).

HABITAT: Clear, cold lakes and reservoirs. Adults generally ascend streams to spawn, but also spawn in gravel and rocky shorelines of lakes with groundwater upwellings.

ORIGIN: Possibly native in Kootenai River Drainage. Introduced elsewhere in Montana. Original range of Kokanee is lakes on the Pacific slope in Alaska, Yukon Territory, British Columbia, Washington, Idaho, and Oregon. Also occurs naturally in Japan and northeast Asia.

COMMENT: The Kokanee is a landlocked Sockeye Salmon—a Pacific salmon. Both sexes die after spawning. Kokanee travel in schools and the growth of individual fish depends on population density. High density results in undesirably small fish due to intense competition for food.

RAINBOW TROUT   and   REDBAND TROUT
Oncorhynchus mykiss   *Oncorhynchus mykiss* subspecies

The Redband Trout is regarded as a subspecies within the "rainbow trout group"; however, it has not yet been officially classified by fisheries scientists. Since it and the Rainbow Trout are similar in appearance they are here treated together. In Montana populations of Native Redband Trout (they are also referred to as Inland or Interior Rainbow Trout) occur only in a few waters of the Kootenai Drainage. It is a fish of special concern.

Rainbow Trout

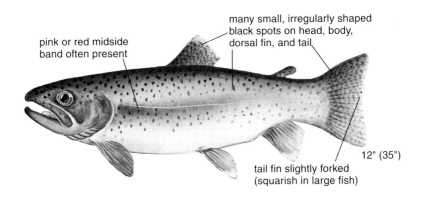

pink or red midside
band often present

many small, irregularly shaped
black spots on head, body,
dorsal fin, and tail

12" (35")

tail fin slightly forked
(squarish in large fish)

OTHER NAMES: Silver (a Rainbow Trout with silvery iridescence is sometimes miscalled a Silver Salmon). Kamloops and Steelhead are strains of Rainbow Trout.

Rainbow
widespread
in ponds

Rainbow Trout
⬭ limit of Redband
Trout

COLOR: The painting on p. 51 and the illustration above typify a Rainbow from a clear stream. Individuals living in large or turbid lakes or under ice tend to be iridescent silver.

OTHER CHARACTERISTICS: The Redband Trout has larger spots and usually a darker background color than the Rainbow Trout. The Redband also has faint cutthroat slashes, may have red-orange hues on the body, and parr marks may persist in adults. However, there is no simple field technique for separating Redband Trout from Rainbow Trout.

SIMILAR SPECIES: (1) Westslope Cutthroat Trout and (2) Yellowstone Cutthroat Trout have distinct red to orange cutthroat slashes and spots concentrated toward the rear with few or none on the snout; they also usually have tiny teeth behind the "tongue." Crosses between the Cutthroat subspecies and Rainbow Trout are common. Genetic analysis is required for positive identification. See (3) Golden Trout, (4) Brown Trout, and (5) Kokanee.

HABITAT: Clear, cool streams and lakes.

ORIGIN: The principal native range of Rainbow Trout is in western North America with a small portion in northeastern Asia. Except for the Redband Trout subspecies, all Rainbow Trout populations in Montana originated from hatchery fish.

WESTSLOPE CUTTHROAT TROUT
Oncorhynchus clarki lewisi
(A subspecies of Cutthroat Trout)

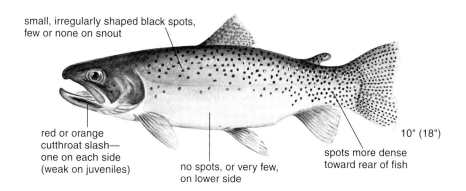

small, irregularly shaped black spots, few or none on snout

red or orange cutthroat slash— one on each side (weak on juveniles)

no spots, or very few, on lower side

spots more dense toward rear of fish

10" (18")

MONTANA STATE FISH (shares this title with Yellowstone Cutthroat Trout).

OTHER NAMES: Flat, Native, Blackspotted Cutthroat Trout, Redbelly, Mountain Trout, Upper Missouri Cutthroat Trout.

COLOR: See p. 51.

OTHER CHARACTERISTICS: Tiny teeth usually present on floor of mouth behind "tongue." These are embedded in tissue and difficult to see but may be felt if brushed with the side of a needle. Lower sides red during spawning season.

distribution of pure-strain Westslope Cutthroat Trout— in Missouri River Basin mostly in high-elevation tributary streams

SIMILAR SPECIES: (1) Yellowstone Cutthroat Trout typically has yellow-brown hues, whereas Westslope is usually silvery steel gray with olive tints on back shading to white underneath. Yellowstone has fewer, larger, and rounder black spots that extend to the lower side. (2) Distinguishing Rainbow Trout from Westslope Cutthrout is difficult since both are silvery with irregularly shaped spots (the Rainbow's are more evenly distributed), both may have a pinkish midside band (usually a Rainbow characteristic), and some Rainbows have a faint yellow to reddish cutthroat slash on each side under the jaw. Crosses between Rainbow Trout and Cutthroat are common. Genetic analysis is required for positive identification. See (3) Golden Trout and (4) Brown Trout.

HABITAT: Clear, cold streams and lakes.

ORIGIN: Native to Montana west of the Continental Divide, and in some drainages east of the divide where it is referred to as Upper Missouri Cutthroat Trout.

COMMENT: Displaced from much of its original range and designated a fish of special concern. Montana Fish, Wildlife & Parks maintains a hatchery brood stock.

YELLOWSTONE CUTTHROAT TROUT
Oncorhynchus clarki bouvieri
(A subspecies of Cutthroat Trout)

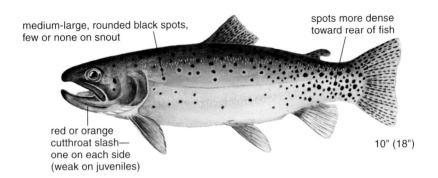

medium-large, rounded black spots, few or none on snout

spots more dense toward rear of fish

red or orange cutthroat slash— one on each side (weak on juveniles)

10" (18")

MONTANA STATE FISH (shares this title with Westslope Cutthroat Trout).

OTHER NAMES: Blackspotted Cutthroat Trout, Blackspotted Trout, Native.

COLOR: See p. 51.

OTHER CHARACTERISTICS: Tiny teeth usually present on floor of mouth behind "tongue." These are embedded in tissue and difficult to see but may be felt if brushed with the side of a needle. Red on side of head and gill cover becomes intense in breeding male.

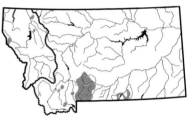

distribution of pure-strain Yellowstone Cutthroat Trout

SIMILAR SPECIES: (1) Rainbow Trout is silvery and usually profusely covered with small, irregularly shaped black spots, whereas the Yellowstone Cutthroat often has a yellow-brown background color and larger, rounder spots concentrated toward the tail. The adult Yellowstone's distinct red or orange cutthroat slash is the most dependable feature for distinguishing it from Rainbow Trout or hybrids in the field. Genetic testing is needed for positive identification. See (2) Westslope Cutthroat Trout, (3) Golden Trout, and (4) Brown Trout.

HABITAT: Clear, cold lakes and streams.

ORIGIN: Native to Montana in Yellowstone River Drainage from Tongue River upstream. Widely distributed due to stocking with hatchery fish.

COMMENT: Because of a continual, significant decline in natural populations, the Yellowstone Cutthroat Trout is designated a fish of special concern. Montana Fish, Wildlife & Parks maintains a brood stock.

GOLDEN TROUT
Oncorhynchus aguabonita

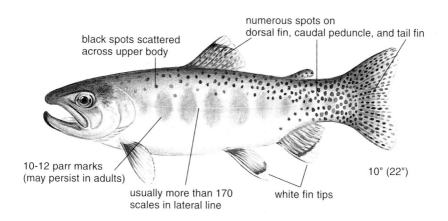

black spots scattered across upper body

numerous spots on dorsal fin, caudal peduncle, and tail fin

10-12 parr marks (may persist in adults)

usually more than 170 scales in lateral line

white fin tips

10" (22")

COLOR: See p. 51.

SIMILAR SPECIES: (1) Rainbow Trout is densely covered with irregularly shaped black spots and usually has 160 or fewer scales in lateral line. (2) Cutthroat Trout has cutthroat slashes, usually has at least a few small teeth behind "tongue," and pelvic and anal fins do not have white tips. (3) Hybrid Golden Trout (Golden Trout crossed with Rainbow Trout or Cutthroat Trout) are found in a number of mountain lakes. Positive identification can be made only by genetic analysis.

HABITAT: In Montana, alpine lakes; also successful in clear, cool lakes at lower elevations.

ORIGIN: Introduced into Montana. Native only to the upper Kern River Basin in California.

COMMENT: Pure-strain Golden Trout are present in about 20 mountain lakes or mountain lake chains in western and south-central Montana. This species is considered by many to be the most beautiful of North American trouts.

BROWN TROUT
Salmo trutta

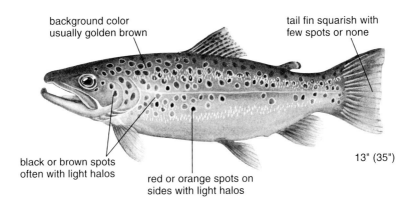

background color
usually golden brown

tail fin squarish with
few spots or none

black or brown spots
often with light halos

red or orange spots on
sides with light halos

13" (35")

OTHER NAMES: Loch Leven Trout, German Brown (Von Behr) Trout.

COLOR: See p. 52.

OTHER CHARACTERISTICS: May lack red and orange spots. Black (or brown) spots may be irregularly shaped or rounded. Spots with halos on gill cover are a clue (if present) that a trout is a Brown Trout. Fish living in large or turbid lakes or under ice acquire a silvery iridescence that often hides most of the spotting.

SIMILAR SPECIES: (1) Brook Trout has wavy lines on back and intense white edge on anal fin and paired fins. (2) Rainbow Trout and (3) Cutthroat Trout have many spots in rows on tail fin, do not have red spots or halos around spots.

HABITAT: Valley streams and rivers; also lakes and reservoirs with suitable spawning tributaries.

ORIGIN: Native to Europe and western Asia; introduced into Montana. The Von Behr and Loch Leven are varieties of Brown Trout brought from Germany and Scotland, respectively. They are now irretrievably mixed.

BROOK TROUT
Salvelinus fontinalis

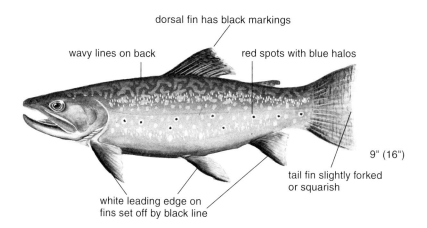

dorsal fin has black markings

wavy lines on back

red spots with blue halos

9" (16")

tail fin slightly forked
or squarish

white leading edge on
fins set off by black line

OTHER NAMES: Eastern Brook Trout, Squaretail.

COLOR: See p. 52.

SIMILAR SPECIES: See (1) Bull Trout, (2) Lake Trout, and (3) Brown Trout. (4) Brook Trout occasionally hybridize with Brown Trout. The offspring, called Tiger Trout, have the markings of a tiger or giraffe. They are very rare since mortality of eggs and newly hatched fish is high and hybrids reaching adulthood are usually sterile.

HABITAT: Clear, cold, well-oxygenated streams and lakes. Prefers small, spring-fed streams and ponds with aquatic vegetation. Often overpopulates, resulting in fish too small to attract fishermen.

ORIGIN: Introduced into Montana. Native in northeastern North America to west side of Hudson Bay and Minnesota, and in the Appalachian Mountains south to Georgia.

Tiger Trout

BULL TROUT
Salvelinus confluentus

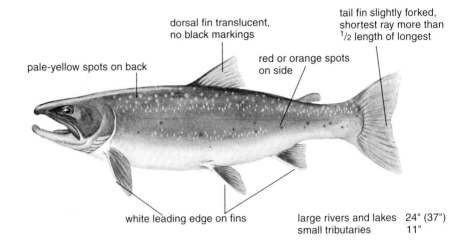

dorsal fin translucent,
no black markings

tail fin slightly forked,
shortest ray more than
$1/2$ length of longest

pale-yellow spots on back

red or orange spots
on side

white leading edge on fins

large rivers and lakes 24" (37")
small tributaries   11"

OTHER NAME: Called Dolly Varden until 1978 when the primarily inland form of Dolly Varden was designated a separate species, the Bull Trout.

COLOR: See p. 52.

SIMILAR SPECIES: (1) Brook Trout has wavy lines on back and black markings on dorsal fin. (2) See Lake Trout.

HABITAT: Primarily large, coldwater streams and lakes; also smaller waters. Lake dwellers ascend streams to spawn.

ORIGIN: Native to Montana.

COMMENT: The Bull Trout is currently found in less than half of the waters it originally inhabited in Montana, and almost half of the remaining populations are at high risk of genetic contamination from Brook Trout. It is therefore a fish of special concern.

LAKE TROUT
Salvelinus namaycush

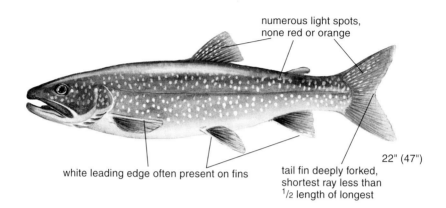

numerous light spots,
none red or orange

white leading edge often present on fins

tail fin deeply forked,
shortest ray less than
$^{1}/_{2}$ length of longest

22" (47")

OTHER NAME: Mackinaw Trout.

COLOR: See p. 52.

OTHER CHARACTERISTICS: May have pale wavy
lines on back. Fins may have traces of orange.

SIMILAR SPECIES: (1) Bull Trout has fewer spots and some
that are orange or red, dark background color does not extend
as far down sides, and tail fin is not as deeply forked. (2) Brook Trout has nearly square tail fin
and red spots with blue halos.

HABITAT: Deep, cold lakes and reservoirs.

ORIGIN: Original range is in parts of Alaska, most of Canada, and northernmost United
States from the Great Lakes to the East Coast. Native to Montana in Elk, Twin, Saint Mary,
and Waterton lakes.

ARCTIC GRAYLING
Thymallus arcticus

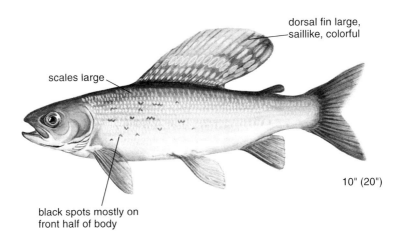

dorsal fin large,
saillike, colorful

scales large

10" (20")

black spots mostly on
front half of body

OTHER NAME: Montana Grayling.

COLOR: See p. 53.

SIMILAR SPECIES: (1) Whitefishes, (2) trouts, and (3) salmons do not have saillike dorsal fin.

HABITAT: Today, in Montana, primarily small, cold, clear lakes with tributaries suitable for spawning. Does not coexist well with other fishes except Cutthroat Trout and others with which it evolved.

ORIGIN: Native range extends from northwestern Canada across Alaska to Eurasia. Also, isolated populations survived the last glaciation south of the ice sheet in present-day Montana, extreme northwestern Wyoming, and Michigan. It is now extinct in Michigan.

COMMENT: About 30 Montana lakes have fishable populations. Historically a stream fish in the Missouri River Drainage upstream from Great Falls, the Arctic Grayling's range has been reduced until the only entirely fluvial (stream) population in Montana is in the Big Hole River Drainage. The fluvial form of Arctic Grayling is a fish of special concern.

MOUNTAIN WHITEFISH
Prosopium williamsoni

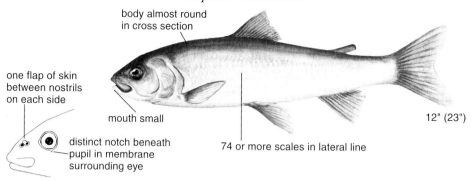

body almost round
in cross section

one flap of skin
between nostrils
on each side

mouth small

distinct notch beneath
pupil in membrane
surrounding eye

74 or more scales in lateral line

12" (23")

OTHER NAME: Rocky Mountain Whitefish.

COLOR: See p. 53.

OTHER CHARACTERISTICS: Mouth overhung by snout.

SIMILAR SPECIES: (1) The largest Pygmy Whitefish is only about 8 inches in length; it has a more rounded snout and fewer scales in lateral line. (2) Trouts and (3) salmons have larger mouth and smaller scales. See (4) Lake Whitefish and (5) Arctic Grayling.

HABITAT: Medium-sized and large, clear, cold rivers; also some lakes and reservoirs.

ORIGIN: Native to Montana.

PYGMY WHITEFISH
Prosopium coulteri

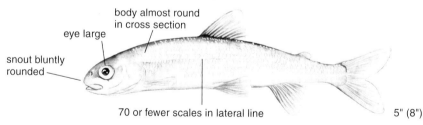

body almost round
in cross section

eye large

snout bluntly
rounded

70 or fewer scales in lateral line

5" (8")

COLOR: Silvery except for olive-brown back.

OTHER CHARACTERISTICS: Mouth overhung by snout. Has one flap of skin between nostrils on each side, and membrane surrounding eye has distinct notch below pupil (see Mountain Whitefish for illustration).

SIMILAR SPECIES: A large eye on a small whitefish is a field clue indicating a Pygmy Whitefish. See (1) Mountain Whitefish and (2) Lake Whitefish.

HABITAT: Deep, cold lakes; adults ascend streams to spawn.

ORIGIN: Native to Montana.

LAKE WHITEFISH
Coregonus clupeaformis

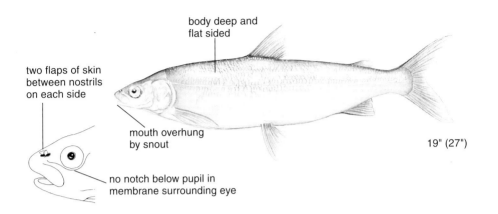

body deep and
flat sided

two flaps of skin
between nostrils
on each side

mouth overhung
by snout

19" (27")

no notch below pupil in
membrane surrounding eye

COLOR: Silvery, with olive to light-brown back.

SIMILAR SPECIES: This is the only Montana white-fish which does not have a distinct notch below pupil in membrane surrounding eye. The Mountain Whitefish and Pygmy Whitefish have nearly round bodies and only one flap of skin between nostrils. See Cisco.

HABITAT: Primarily deep, clear, cold lakes where it is found mostly at depths of 50 to 90 feet. Comes into shallower water to spawn, rarely ascends tributary streams. Has thrived in Fresno Reservoir, a shallow, warm, often-turbid reservoir.

ORIGIN: Native to the Great Lakes, some New England Lakes, and lakes all across Canada and Alaska. May be native to Saint Mary Lake in Glacier National Park.

CISCO
Coregonus artedi

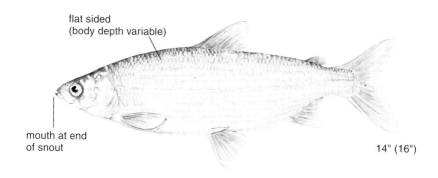

flat sided
(body depth variable)

mouth at end
of snout

14" (16")

OTHER NAMES: Lake Herring, Tullibee.

COLOR: Silvery, somewhat darker on back.

OTHER CHARACTERISTICS: Lower jaw often pro-
trudes slightly with mouth closed, but jaws may be equal or
upper may be slightly longer. Has 38 or more gill rakers on
first arch, two flaps of skin between nostrils (see Lake Whitefish for illustration), and membrane surrounding eye has distinct notch below pupil (see Mountain Whitefish for illustration).

SIMILAR SPECIES: Other Montana whitefishes have a less sharp snout that overhangs mouth,
and 33 or fewer gill rakers on first arch.

HABITAT: Large, cold, clear lakes.

ORIGIN: Introduced into Montana. Native to north-central and northeastern United States
and most of Canada.

COMMENT: A reproducing population has become established in Fort Peck Lake as the
result of heavy planting from 1984 to 1986. It was introduced as forage for sport fishes.

TROUT-PERCH FAMILY
Percopsidae

Trout-perches have characteristics of both the trout and perch families. They have an adipose fin like the trouts and yet have spines in some fins and superficially resemble members of the perch family. One species occurs in Montana.

TROUT-PERCH
Percopsis omiscomaycus

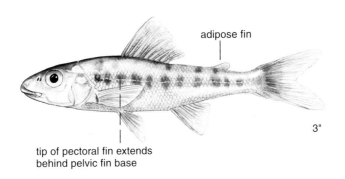

adipose fin

tip of pectoral fin extends
behind pelvic fin base

3"

COLOR: Silvery with translucent effect; dark spots in rows on upper half of body.

OTHER CHARACTERISTICS: Dorsal and anal fins have weak spines. Teeth are small and in brushlike bands.

SIMILAR SPECIES: In (1) Rainbow Smelt and (2) members of trout family tip of pectoral fin does not extend behind front of pelvic fin. (3) Members of perch family lack an adipose fin.

HABITAT: Typically lakes but also clear to moderately turbid streams, particularly when spawning.

ORIGIN: Native in Montana and in a broad band extending southeastward from Alaska across much of Canada to Kansas and West Virginia. Currently the only Montana records are for Lower Saint Mary Lake and associated Saint Mary Canal; therefore, it is a fish of special concern.

BULLHEAD CATFISH FAMILY
Ictaluridae

This family is characterized by scaleless fishes with eight long "cat's whiskers" (barbels), an adipose fin, and a sharp spine at the front of the dorsal and each pectoral fin. In some species the pectoral spines have a sawlike rear edge.

CHANNEL CATFISH

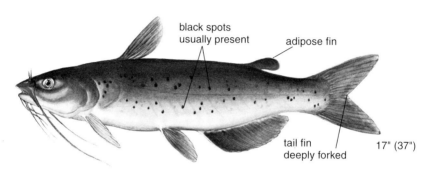

black spots usually present

adipose fin

tail fin deeply forked

17" (37")

Ictalurus punctatus

COLOR: See p. 53.

SIMILAR SPECIES: Other Montana catfishes do not have a deeply forked tail fin.

HABITAT: Large rivers and lowland lakes. Thrives at water temperatures above 70° F. Tolerates turbid water.

ORIGIN: Native to Montana.

BLACK BULLHEAD
Ameiurus melas

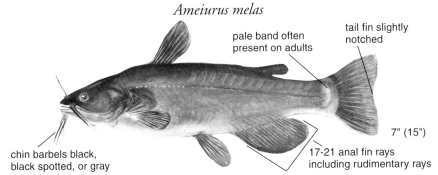

pale band often present on adults

tail fin slightly notched

chin barbels black, black spotted, or gray

7" (15")

17-21 anal fin rays including rudimentary rays

COLOR: See p. 53.

OTHER CHARACTERISTICS: Rear edge of spine in pectoral fins smooth or nearly so. Membranes between fin rays darker than rays.

SIMILAR SPECIES: (1) Yellow Bullhead has white or light-colored chin barbels (no black pigment) and 24 or more rays in anal fin. See (2) Stonecat and (3) Channel Catfish.

HABITAT: Turbid, mud-bottomed lakes and ponds; also pools and backwaters of streams. Tolerates high water temperatures and low levels of dissolved oxygen.

ORIGIN: Native in central and eastern North America west of the Appalachian Mountains from southern Canada to the Gulf Coast. Probably not native to Montana.

YELLOW BULLHEAD
Ameiurus natalis

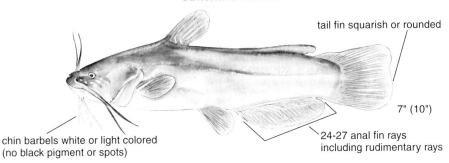

tail fin squarish or rounded

chin barbels white or light colored (no black pigment or spots)

7" (10")

24-27 anal fin rays including rudimentary rays

COLOR: Overall yellowish brown to yellow, back darker, underside yellow or white. Young usually dark brown or black, with light-colored underside.

OTHER CHARACTERISTICS: Rear edge of spine in pectoral fins has sawlike teeth.

SIMILAR SPECIES: See (1) Black Bullhead, (2) Stonecat, and (3) Channel Catfish.

HABITAT: Weedy, shallow, clear-water areas of lakes and slow-moving streams.

ORIGIN: Introduced into Montana. Native in eastern North America as far west as eastern North Dakota and from the Great Lakes to the Gulf of Mexico.

STONECAT
Noturus flavus

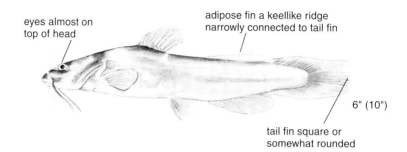

eyes almost on top of head

adipose fin a keellike ridge narrowly connected to tail fin

6" (10")

tail fin square or somewhat rounded

COLOR: Overall yellowish brown, back darker, underside light yellow or white.

SIMILAR SPECIES: (1) Other Montana catfishes have flaplike adipose fin that is free at posterior end. In addition, Channel Catfish has forked tail fin. (2) See Burbot.

HABITAT: Swift-water areas of streams among rocks or under logs; also lakes over sand and gravel bottom where there is wave action.

ORIGIN: Native to Montana.

COMMENT: Handle Stonecats carefully; spines in their fins have well-developed poison glands that can inflict a beelike sting. Ordinarily this is not dangerous.

CODFISH FAMILY
Gadidae

Codfishes have long bodies. All fins are soft rayed and the pelvic fins are located far forward. The Burbot is the only freshwater member of this family.

BURBOT
Lota lota

long eellike body

second dorsal fin long

single chin barbel

anal fin long

tail fin rounded

20" (39")

OTHER NAME: Ling.

COLOR: See p. 54.

OTHER CHARACTERISTICS: Skin appears smooth, but tiny embedded scales are present.

SIMILAR SPECIES: Montana members of the bullhead catfish family have eight barbels and pelvic fins are placed much farther back on body.

HABITAT: Large rivers; cold, deep lakes and reservoirs.

ORIGIN: Native to Montana.

STICKLEBACK FAMILY
Gasterosteidae

Sticklebacks are small fishes with a series of separate spines on the back in front of a soft-rayed dorsal fin. There is one representative of this family in Montana waters.

BROOK STICKLEBACK
Culaea inconstans

5 spines (rarely 4 or 6) on back

pelvic fin small
(one spine and one soft ray)

2" (2^1/$_2$")

COLOR: Olive green with mottling or light spots on sides; underside light yellow to silver. During breeding season males are black with tinges of red; females may be dusky.

OTHER CHARACTERISTICS: Body smooth, without scales, but with minute bony plates about the pores on the lateral line.

HABITAT: Associated with dense vegetation in slow, clear streams and shallow lakes.

ORIGIN: Native to Montana.

SUNFISH FAMILY
Centrarchidae

This family contains not only the sunfishes and Rock Bass, but also the crappies and black basses (they are not actually black). The dorsal fin has spiny- and soft-rayed portions which are broadly (or, in the black basses, narrowly) joined into a single fin. The paired fins are nearly one above the other.

BLACK CRAPPIE
Pomoxis nigromaculatus

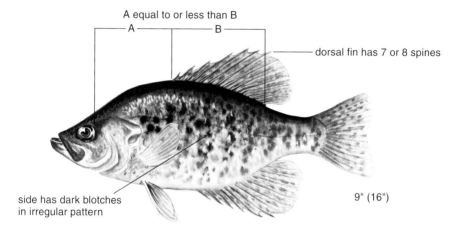

A equal to or less than B

dorsal fin has 7 or 8 spines

side has dark blotches in irregular pattern

9" (16")

OTHER NAME: Calico Bass.

COLOR: See p. 54.

OTHER CHARACTERISTICS: Fish from turbid water may be lighter colored.

SIMILAR SPECIES: White Crappie's dorsal fin has a shorter base, is set farther back, and has 5 or 6 spines (rarely 7) compared with the Black Crappie's 7 or 8. White Crappie has vague vertical bands on sides.

HABITAT: Ponds, lakes, reservoirs, and slow portions of streams. Prefers clear water and abundant cover such as submerged timber or aquatic vegetation.

ORIGIN: Introduced into Montana. Native in central and eastern North America west of the Appalachian Mountains from southern Canada to the Gulf Coast, and north on the Atlantic Coast from Florida to Virginia.

WHITE CRAPPIE
Pomoxis annularis

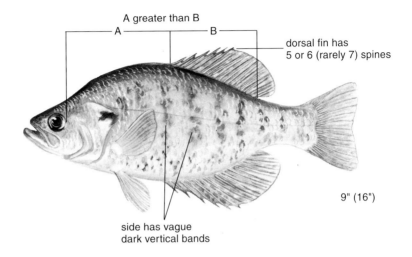

A greater than B

A ———— B

dorsal fin has
5 or 6 (rarely 7) spines

9" (16")

side has vague
dark vertical bands

COLOR: See p. 54.

SIMILAR SPECIES: See Black Crappie.

HABITAT: Ponds, lakes, and reservoirs and slow portions of streams. Seeks weedy areas, logs, and other protective cover. Seems more tolerant of turbid water than Black Crappie.

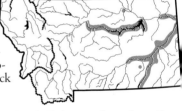

ORIGIN: Introduced into Montana. Native from eastern South Dakota and southern Great Lakes region to the Gulf Coast from Texas to Alabama.

PUMPKINSEED
Lepomis gibbosus

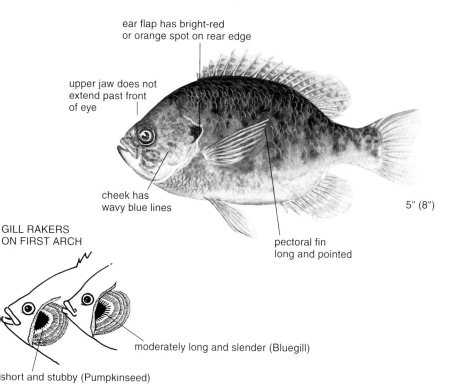

ear flap has bright-red or orange spot on rear edge

upper jaw does not extend past front of eye

cheek has wavy blue lines

pectoral fin long and pointed

5" (8")

GILL RAKERS ON FIRST ARCH

moderately long and slender (Bluegill)

short and stubby (Pumpkinseed)

drawing by Vern Craig

OTHER NAME: Common Sunfish.

COLOR: See p. 54.

OTHER CHARACTERISTICS: Gill rakers short and stubby (see illustration).

SIMILAR SPECIES: (1) Bluegill has completely black ear flap, longer gill rakers, and black blotch on rear of dorsal fin. See (2) Green Sunfish and (3) Rock Bass.

HABITAT: Ponds, small lakes, margins of large lakes, and slow streams. Prefers areas with aquatic vegetation and submerged brush.

ORIGIN: Introduced into Montana. Native to north-central and eastern North America.

BLUEGILL
Lepomis macrochirus

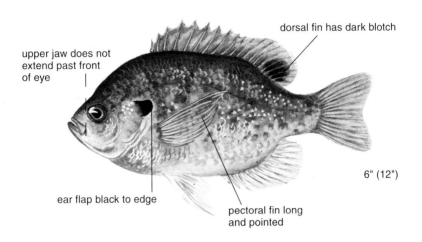

upper jaw does not extend past front of eye

dorsal fin has dark blotch

ear flap black to edge

pectoral fin long and pointed

6" (12")

OTHER NAME: Bluegill Sunfish.

COLOR: See p. 55.

OTHER CHARACTERISTICS: Gill rakers moderately long and slender (see p. 79 for illustration). Ear flap smaller on females and young males than on adult males. Young usually have vertical bars on sides that become faint on adults.

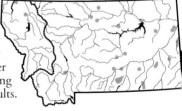

SIMILAR SPECIES: See (1) Pumpkinseed, (2) Green Sunfish, and (3) Rock Bass.

HABITAT: Areas of aquatic vegetation in comparatively warm ponds and lakes; slow, weed streams.

ORIGIN: Introduced into Montana. Original range was from southern Canada through east ern, central, and southern United States including Texas.

COMMENT: The name bluegill comes from the bluish color on the lower part of the gi cover.

GREEN SUNFISH
Lepomis cyanellus

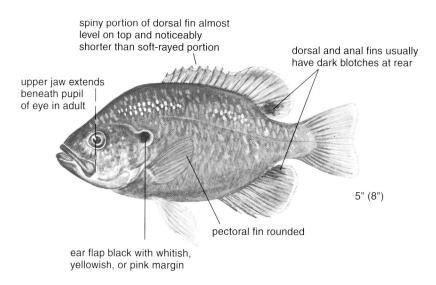

spiny portion of dorsal fin almost level on top and noticeably shorter than soft-rayed portion

dorsal and anal fins usually have dark blotches at rear

upper jaw extends beneath pupil of eye in adult

5" (8")

pectoral fin rounded

ear flap black with whitish, yellowish, or pink margin

COLOR: See p. 55.

OTHER CHARACTERISTICS: Body robust. Gill rakers long and slender. Breeding males have light-colored fringe on dorsal, anal, and tail fins.

SIMILAR SPECIES: (1) Bluegill and (2) Pumpkinseed have smaller mouth and pointed, usually longer, pectoral fins. Bluegill has completely black ear flap; Pumpkinseed has short, stubby gill rakers. Both are usually deeper bodied than the Green Sunfish. (3) See Rock Bass.

HABITAT: Slow-moving streams at lower elevations and shallows of lakes. Tolerates turbid water, high temperatures, and low dissolved oxygen.

ORIGIN: Introduced into Montana. Original range includes much of central and eastern North America west of the Appalachian Mountains from the Great Lakes region south to Georgia and northeastern Mexico.

ROCK BASS
Ambloplites rupestris

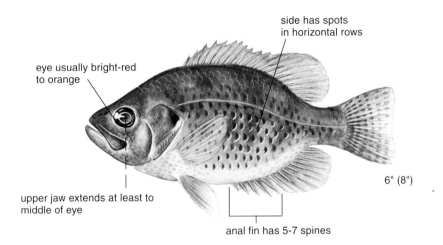

eye usually bright-red to orange

side has spots in horizontal rows

upper jaw extends at least to middle of eye

anal fin has 5-7 spines

6" (8")

OTHER NAMES: Redeye, Goggle Eye.

COLOR: See p. 55.

OTHER CHARACTERISTICS: Body robust.

SIMILAR SPECIES: (1) Pumpkinseed, (2) Bluegill, and (3) Green Sunfish lack the red eye and rows of spots on the side, and have only 3 spines in the anal fin.

HABITAT: Pools of rocky-bottomed streams; rocky, shallow areas of lakes. Seeks moderately warm water. In Montana found only in Tongue River Drainage.

ORIGIN: Native range is from southern Canada as far west as Manitoba, through central and eastern United States to Alabama and Georgia. Was introduced into the Tongue River in Wyoming and moved downstream into Montana.

SMALLMOUTH BASS
Micropterus dolomieu

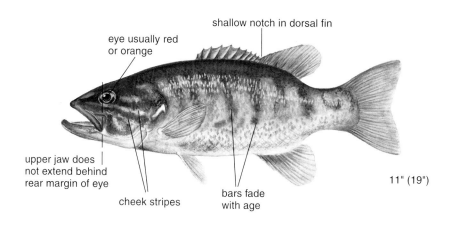

eye usually red
or orange

shallow notch in dorsal fin

upper jaw does
not extend behind
rear margin of eye

cheek stripes

bars fade
with age

11" (19")

OTHER NAMES: Northern Smallmouth Bass, Smallmouth Black Bass, Bronze-back.

COLOR: See p. 55.

OTHER CHARACTERISTICS: Length of longest dor-
sal spine is less than twice the length of shortest dorsal spine
at notch. Young have tricolored tail fin with yellow or orange innermost, a dark vertical band in center, and a whitish
outer edge.

SIMILAR SPECIES: See Largemouth Bass.

HABITAT: Over boulders and to lesser extent over gravel in cool, clear lakes and streams.

ORIGIN: Introduced to Montana. Native from Minnesota to Quebec and southward to Okla-
homa and Alabama.

LARGEMOUTH BASS
Micropterus salmoides

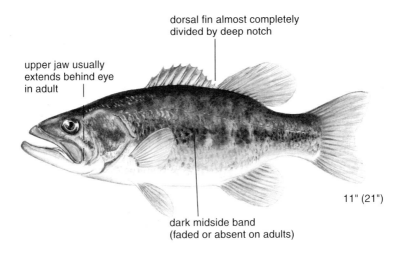

dorsal fin almost completely
divided by deep notch

upper jaw usually
extends behind eye
in adult

11" (21")

dark midside band
(faded or absent on adults)

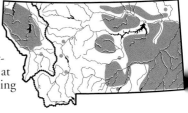

OTHER NAME: Largemouth Black Bass.

COLOR: See p. 56.

OTHER CHARACTERISTICS: Length of longest dorsal spine at least twice the length of shortest dorsal spine at notch. Young have a bicolored tail fin, the rear part being darker than the forward part.

SIMILAR SPECIES: Smallmouth Bass has a smaller mouth and a broader connection between spiny- and soft-rayed portions of dorsal fin. It is more streamlined, tends to brownish hue (Largemouth to blackish), has prominent stripes on cheek, and lacks dark midside band that is so prominent on young Largemouth.

HABITAT: Clear, mud-bottomed lakes and stream backwaters. Seeks areas with comparatively warm summer water temperatures and ample aquatic vegetation.

ORIGIN: Introduced into Montana. Native from southeastern Canada southward through the Great Lakes and Mississippi Valley to the Gulf Coast, and north on the Atlantic Coast from Florida to Virginia.

DRUM FAMILY
Sciaenidae

Drums are basslike, spiny-rayed fishes that are unique in having the lateral line extend onto the tail fin. Montana has one representative of this family.

FRESHWATER DRUM
Aplodinotus grunniens

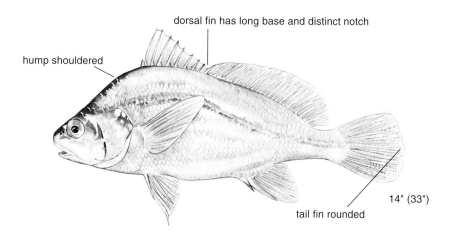

hump shouldered

dorsal fin has long base and distinct notch

tail fin rounded

14" (33")

OTHER NAME: Sheepshead.

COLOR: Silvery with a pearl-gray back.

OTHER CHARACTERISTICS: This is the only Montana fish in which the lateral line extends onto the tail fin.

HABITAT: Large streams, large lakes, and reservoirs.

ORIGIN: Native to Montana.

COMMENT: The Drum's unusually large otoliths (ear bones) are ivorylike and prized as "lucky bones." This fish is named for the drumming sound, heard mostly during the summer, produced by special muscles acting on the air bladder.

SCULPIN FAMILY
Cottidae

Sculpins are small, bottom-dwelling, spiny-rayed (spines are weak) fishes with large, flattened heads and fanlike pectoral fins. The long dorsal fin has a spiny-rayed portion and a soft-rayed portion which are usually narrowly divided. Scales are absent or reduced, and in many species the body is partly covered with prickles.

These fishes are variable in structure and color, often making identification perplexing even for fisheries biologists. The development of palatine teeth is useful in separating some species. They are in the roof of the mouth on a pair of bones that extend outward and rearward on each side as shown below.

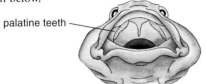

palatine teeth

Adapted from: J.D. McPhail and C.C. Lindsey, *Freshwater Fishes of Northwestern Canada and Alaska*, Fish. Res. Bd. Canada Bull. 173, 1970, p. 316.

The presence of palatine teeth may be determined by carefully brushing the area where they should occur with the side of a needle. Care should be taken not to mistake other teeth on the roof of the mouth for the palatines.

MOTTLED SCULPIN
Cottus bairdi

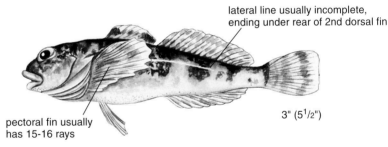

lateral line usually incomplete, ending under rear of 2nd dorsal fin

pectoral fin usually has 15-16 rays

3" (5¹/2")

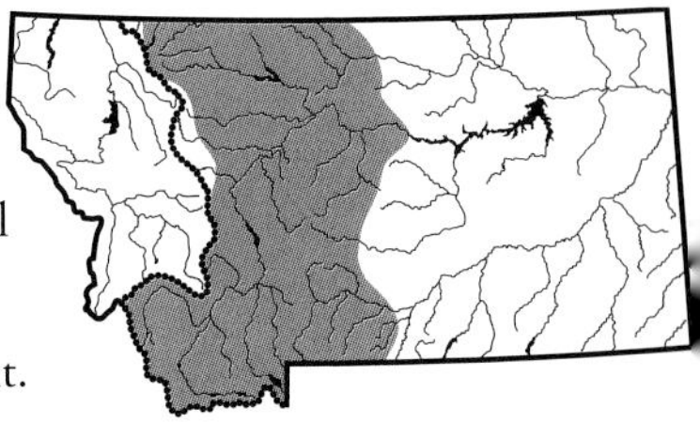

3" (5$^1/_2$")

OTHER NAMES: Bullhead, Muddler.

COLOR: Back and sides slate to brown with mottling and dark blotches. May have two or three dark saddles under second dorsal fin. Underside whitish. First dorsal fin fringed with orange or red on breeding males.

OTHER CHARACTERISTICS: Palatine teeth present.

SIMILAR SPECIES: (1) Shorthead Sculpin (see COMMENT below) usually has 13 to 14 pectoral fin rays, compared with Mottled's usual 15 to 16. In Montana the Shorthead is in the Columbia River Drainage, whereas the Mottled is in the Missouri, Yellowstone, and Saint Mary river drainages. (2) See Slimy Sculpin.

HABITAT: Cold streams; to a lesser extent, rocky shorelines of lakes.

ORIGIN: Native to Montana.

COMMENT: The Mottled and Shorthead sculpins are similar in physical and biological characteristics. Fisheries scientists have yet to determine if they are varieties of the same species.

SHORTHEAD SCULPIN
Cottus confusus

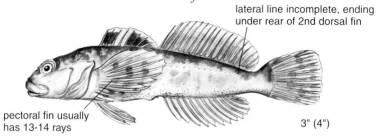

lateral line incomplete, ending under rear of 2nd dorsal fin

pectoral fin usually has 13-14 rays

3" (4")

OTHER NAME: Bullhead.

COLOR: Overall brownish to dusky, mottled. Underside light with fine speckles.

OTHER CHARACTERISTICS: Palatine teeth present in short, narrow row not easily seen.

SIMILAR SPECIES: See (1) Mottled Sculpin (including COMMENT on p. 86) and (2) Slimy Sculpin.

HABITAT: Riffles of small, cold, clear streams; sometimes found in large streams.

ORIGIN: Native to Montana.

COMMENT: Reported from only a few Montana streams and designated a fish of special concern.

SLIMY SCULPIN
Cottus cognatus

lateral line incomplete, ending under center of 2nd dorsal fin

skin slimy, almost no prickles

3" (4")

OTHER NAME: Bullhead.

COLOR: Back and sides brown to black with mottling, dark bands often present. Underside white. First dorsal fin fringed with orange on breeding males.

OTHER CHARACTERISTICS: No palatine teeth. Pelvic fin has 3 or 4 soft rays; if a fourth (inner) ray is present, it is usually two-thirds or less the length of the longest. Other Montana sculpins have 4 fully developed soft rays. Note: Sculpin pelvic fins have 1 spine in addition to the soft rays. It is encased in a fleshy membrane with the first (outer) ray and is not distinct.

SIMILAR SPECIES: (1) Mottled Sculpin and (2) Shorthead Sculpin have palatine teeth.

HABITAT: Rocky riffles of cold, clear streams; also stony shallows in clear lakes.

ORIGIN: Native to Montana.

TORRENT SCULPIN
Cottus rhotheus

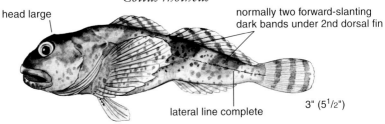

head large

normally two forward-slanting dark bands under 2nd dorsal fin

lateral line complete

3" (5^1/$_2$")

OTHER NAME: Bullhead.

COLOR: Gray brown with black speckling. Underside light, chin strongly mottled. First dorsal fin fringed with orange on spawning male.

OTHER CHARACTERISTICS: Palatine teeth present. Body robust. Usually has coarse prickles on back, sides, and sometimes on caudal peduncle.

SIMILAR SPECIES: Torrent Sculpin is told from other Montana sculpins by its large head, strongly mottled chin, and distinctly forward-slanting dark bands on sides.

HABITAT: Riffles of cold, clear streams; to a lesser extent, the rocky shoals of large lakes.

ORIGIN: Native to Montana.

SPOONHEAD SCULPIN
Cottus ricei

upper spine on gill cover long, curved upward and inward like a bison's horn

head wide and flat

lateral line complete

3" (4")

OTHER NAME: Bullhead.

COLOR: Light brown with two to four saddles under second dorsal fin. Underside whitish.

OTHER CHARACTERISTICS: No palatine teeth. Body slender. One pore on midline under tip of chin. Prickles often dense (may cover entire body), but sometimes sparse or absent.

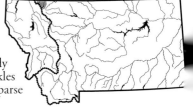

SIMILAR SPECIES: No other Montana sculpin has the "bison horn" spine on gill cover, and the others have two pores under tip of chin.

HABITAT: Small, swift streams to larger rivers; shallows and deep water of lakes.

ORIGIN: Naturally distributed from northwestern Canada to Great Lakes region. In Montana known only from Glacier National Park until 1986, when one was removed from the stomach of a Lake Trout caught in Lower Saint Mary Lake just outside the eastern park boundary.

COMMENT: Designated a fish of special concern due to its limited distribution in Montana.

TEMPERATE BASS FAMILY
Percichthyidae

These are slab-sided, moderately deep-bodied, spiny-rayed fishes with numerous teeth and strong jaws. The first dorsal fin is entirely separate from the second or slightly joined at the base, and there are three spines in the anal fin.

WHITE BASS
Morone chrysops

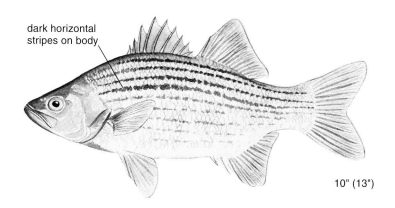

dark horizontal stripes on body

10" (13")

COLOR: Silvery with five to seven dark horizontal stripes on side. Eye tinted with yellow.

SIMILAR SPECIES: No other Montana spiny-rayed fish has horizontal stripes on its side.

HABITAT: Deep pools in rivers and open water of large, clear lakes and reservoirs.

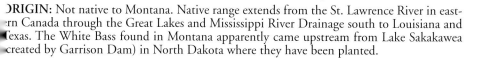

ORIGIN: Not native to Montana. Native range extends from the St. Lawrence River in eastern Canada through the Great Lakes and Mississippi River Drainage south to Louisiana and Texas. The White Bass found in Montana apparently came upstream from Lake Sakakawea (created by Garrison Dam) in North Dakota where they have been planted.

PERCH FAMILY
Percidae

These spiny-rayed fishes have two well-separated dorsal fins—the front one has spines, and the rear one has all or almost all soft rays. The paired fins are nearly one above the other.

YELLOW PERCH
Perca flavescens

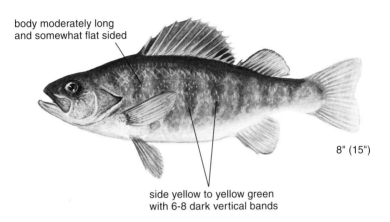

body moderately long
and somewhat flat sided

8" (15")

side yellow to yellow green
with 6-8 dark vertical bands

OTHER NAME: Perch.

COLOR: See p. 56.

OTHER CHARACTERISTICS: Many small teeth but no canine teeth. Anal fin has 2 spines and 6 to 8 soft rays. Lower fins reddish orange in breeding males.

SIMILAR SPECIES: (1) Young Walleye or Sauger might be mistaken for small Yellow Perch. The former two have large canine or tearing teeth, and 11 to 14 soft rays in the anal fin. See (2) Iowa Darter.

HABITAT: Warm to cool, clear lakes with moderate amount of vegetation; to a lesser extent slow, weedy streams.

ORIGIN: Introduced into Montana. Original range is from Great Slave Lake to Nova Scotia in Canada, south through north-central and northeastern United States, and along the Atlantic Coast to South Carolina.

WALLEYE
Stizostedion vitreum

cheek has few
or no scales

first dorsal fin
has dark blotch

16" (33")

outer margin of anal fin and
lower tip of tail fin white

OTHER NAMES: Wall-eyed Pike, Yellow Pikeperch.

COLOR: See p. 56.

OTHER CHARACTERISTICS: Jaws and roof of mouth
have large canine teeth. Anal fin has 2 spines and 11 to 14
(usually 12 or 13) soft rays. Body often has golden hue.

SIMILAR SPECIES: See (1) Sauger, (2) Yellow Perch, and
(3) Iowa Darter.

HABITAT: Primarily large lakes and reservoirs; to a lesser extent, rivers.

ORIGIN: Introduced into Montana. Native to much of Canada and central and eastern United
States.

SAUGER
Stizostedion canadense

cheek mostly scaled

first dorsal fin has rows of rounded spots

lower edge of
tail fin white

13" (28")

OTHER NAME: Sand Pike.

COLOR: See p. 56.

OTHER CHARACTERISTICS: Jaws and roof of mouth
have large canine teeth. Body almost round in cross section. Anal fin has 2 spines and 11 to 14 (usually 12 or 13)
soft rays. Body often has grayish hue with dark blotches.

SIMILAR SPECIES: (1) Walleye has large, dark spot at rear of first dorsal fin; lower lobe of
tail fin has white tip; cheeks have few scales if any. Walleye and Sauger are known to hybridize
in Montana. The hybrid is known as Saugeye. There is no simple field technique to distinguish it from parent stocks. See (2) Yellow Perch and (3) Iowa Darter.

HABITAT: Rivers; shallows of lakes and reservoirs. Seems to prefer turbid water.

ORIGIN: Native to Montana.

IOWA DARTER
Etheostoma exile

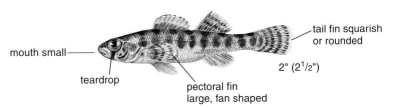

mouth small

teardrop

pectoral fin large, fan shaped

tail fin squarish or rounded

2" (2½")

COLOR: Overall greenish or brownish with about 8 saddle bands across back and 9 to 12 dark blotches on side. In breeding males these blotches become bluish green with rust red between them. The underside becomes orange and the first dorsal fin has a reddish band between a blue base and blue outer edge.

OTHER CHARACTERISTICS: Body slender, eye large, lateral line incomplete.

SIMILAR SPECIES: Could be mistaken for young Yellow Perch, Walleye, or Sauger; however, these have a forked tail fin (well forked on Walleye and Sauger, slightly forked on Yellow Perch) and lack the teardrop marking under the eye.

HABITAT: Clear, weedy, slow-moving streams and shallows of lakes.

ORIGIN: Native to Montana.

COMMENT: One of our smallest native fishes, the Iowa Darter is a bottom dweller. It moves by short, quick dashes, hence the name "darter."

SPAWNING SEASONS

Both water temperature and day length are important in controlling the reproductive rhythm of seasonal spawners. Typical spawning seasons for Montana fishes are:

SPRING
Rainbow Trout
Cutthroat Trout
Arctic Grayling
Northern Pike
Goldeye
Smallmouth Bass
Rock Bass
White Bass
Crappies
Yellow Perch
Walleye
Sauger
Iowa Darter
Rainbow Smelt
Freshwater Drum
Shortnose Gar

Sculpin Family
Brook Stickleback
Central Mudminnow

SPRING or SUMMER
Golden Trout
Largemouth Bass
Sunfishes
Paddlefish
Sturgeon Family
Bullhead Catfish Family
Sucker Family
Minnow Family
Plains Killifish
Trout-Perch

FALL
Brown Trout
Brook Trout
Bull Trout
Lake Trout
Kokanee[1]
Chinook Salmon
Whitefishes
(including Cisco

WINTER
Burbot

[1]*Pacific salmon die after spawning*

PROCEDURE FOR HAVING A FISH DECLARED A STATE RECORD

Montana Fish, Wildlife & Parks administers the record fish program.

There are three requirements for having a fish declared a record:

1. It must be legally caught in Montana.

2. It should be weighed before witnesses on a government-inspected scale such as those found in most grocery stores, and the weight should be certified by a department employee. If a department employee is not present, an affidavit from the store will suffice. The fish's length—measured from the tip of the snout to the farthest tip of the tail fin—is also desirable information; it, too, should be certified by a department employee or other witness.

3. Identification must be verified by a qualified person, preferably a department employee. For some species a good photograph will suffice.

Give the information to a department employee or send it to Conservation Education Division, Montana Fish, Wildlife & Parks, 1420 E. Sixth Avenue, Helena, MT 59620

Drawing by Vern Craig

MONTANA'S RECORD-SETTING FISH (THROUGH 1995)

SPECIES	WEIGHT	ANGLER	YEAR	LOCATION
Arctic Grayling	3.21 lbs.	Frederick C. Dahl	1994	Handkerchief Lake
Bigmouth Buffalo	57.75 lbs.	Craig D. Grassel	1994	Nelson Reservoir
Black Bullhead	2.33 lbs.	Darwin Zempel, Jr.	1994	Lower Flathead River
Black Crappie	3.13 lbs.	Al Elser	1973	Tongue River Reservoir
Blue Sucker	11.46 lbs.	Doug Askin	1989	Yellowstone River (near Miles City)
Bluegill	2.64 lbs.	Brent Fladmo	1983	Peterson's Stock Dam
Brook Trout	9.06 lbs.	John R. Cook	1940	Lower Two Medicine Lake
Brown Trout	29.00 lbs.	E.H. "Peck" Bacon	1966	Wade Lake
Bull Trout	25.63 lbs.	James Hyer	1916	unknown
Burbot (ling)	17.08 lbs.	Jeff E. Iwen	1989	Missouri River (near Wolf Point)
Channel Catfish	25.89 lbs.	Gordon Wentworth	1984	Fort Peck Lake
		Tom Hilderman (tie)	1988	Fort Peck Lake
Chinook Salmon	31.13 lbs.	Carl L. Niles	1991	Fort Peck Lake
Cisco	1.46 lbs.	Jim Liebelt	1990	Fort Peck Trout Pond
Coho Salmon	4.88 lbs.	Irven Strohl	1973	Fort Peck Lake
Common Carp	38.50 lbs.	Don Bagley	1986	Eyraud Lakes
Cutthroat Trout	16.00 lbs.	William D. Sands	1955	Red Eagle Lake
Flathead Chub	0.30 lbs.	Darren Johnson	1995	Missouri River (near Fred Robinson Bridge)
Freshwater Drum	20.44 lbs.	Richard C. Lee	1987	Fort Peck Lake
Golden Trout	4.90 lbs.	Carl Radonski	1993	Lightning Lake
Goldeye	2.91 lbs.	Vance "Bubba" Kielb	1989	Irrigation canal (west of Malta)
Green Sunfish	0.56 lbs.	Roger Fliger	1991	Castle Rock Reservoir
Kokanee (salmon)	5.94 lbs.	Forrest Johnson	1976	Pishkun Reservoir
Lake Trout	42.00 lbs.	Dave Larson	1979	Flathead Lake
Lake Whitefish	10.00 lbs.	Ruby Mutch	1986	Lower St. Mary Lake
		Irwin A. Fanning	1984	Milnor Lake

Species	Angler	Location	Year	Weight
		Marias River (at Loma)		
Mountain Whitefish	Mervin "Frog" Fenimore	Kootenai River (near Libby Dam)	1987	5.09 lbs.
Northern Pike	Lance Moyler	Tongue River Reservoir	1972	37.50 lbs.
Northern Squawfish	Darrel Torgrimson	Noxon Rapids Reservoir	1991	7.88 lbs.
Paddlefish	Larry Branstetter	Missouri River (near Fred Robinson Bridge)	1973	142.50 lbs.
Pallid Sturgeon	Gene Sattler	Yellowstone River (near Sidney)	1979	60.00 lbs.
Peamouth	Gordon Stewart	Ashley Creek	1991	0.64 lbs.
Pumpkinseed	Tim Colver	Milnor Lake	1985	0.95 lbs.
Pygmy Whitefish	Orlin Iverson	Ashley Lake	1982	0.16 lbs.
Rainbow Trout	Stanley Ross	Kootenai River (David Thompson Bridge)	1991	29.02 lbs.
Rainbow-Cutthroat Hybrid	Pat Kelly	Ashley Lake	1982	30.25 lbs.
River Carpsucker	James Jessen	Yellowstone River (near Terry)	1991	3.50 lbs.
Rock Bass	Don Holzheimer	Tongue River Reservoir	1989	0.57 lbs.
Sauger	Gene Moore	Fort Peck Lake	1994	8.81 lbs.
Saugeye	Myron Kibler	Fort Peck Lake	1995	15.66 lbs.
Shorthead Redhorse (sucker)	Ray Quigley	Marias River (near Loma)	1985	4.68 lbs.
Shortnose Gar	John Johnson	Fort Peck dredge cuts	1977	3.06 lbs.
Shovelnose Sturgeon	Sidney L. Storm	Missouri River (near Virgelle)	1986	13.72 lbs.
Smallmouth Bass	Terry L. Druyvestein	Fort Peck Lake	1990	6.09 lbs.
Smallmouth Buffalo	Richard Liesener	Nelson Reservoir	1994	32.63 lbs.
Stonecat	Robert M. Garwood	Milk River (at Havre)	1985	0.42 lbs.
Tiger Muskellunge	Dan Dupea	Lebo Lake	1994	27.00 lbs.
Utah Chub	Eugene Bastian	Canyon Ferry Lake	1992	1.81 lbs.
Walleye	Randy Townsend	Fort Peck Lake	1995	16.29 lbs.
White Bass	Ludwig Dubbe	Fort Peck dredge cuts	1986	1.13 lbs.
White Crappie	Edward Field	Tongue River Reservoir	1995	2.44 lbs.
White Sturgeon	Herb Stout	Kootenai River	1968	96.00 lbs.
White Sucker	Fred Perry	Nelson Reservoir	1983	5.33 lbs.
Yellow Bullhead	Wade Fredenberg	Yellowstone River (near Custer)	1987	0.72 lbs.
Yellow Perch	Vernon Schmid	Ashley Lake	1988	2.37 lbs.

ANSWERS TO COMMONLY ASKED QUESTIONS

QUESTION: Did migrating sea-run salmon or Steelhead ever reach Montana?

ANSWER: Fisheries scientists have scoured published and unpublished records of the historical spawning areas of Pacific salmons and Steelhead (Rainbow Trout that go to sea when young and return to freshwater to spawn), and there is no evidence that these fishes reached Montana, at least not since the last glaciation. Their migrations were evidently blocked by waterfalls. However, White Sturgeon and Redband Trout (also referred to as Inland or Interior Rainbow Trout) occur naturally in Montana's portion of the Kootenai River Drainage downstream from Kootenai Falls. Both had their origins on the Pacific Coast, and the fact they are in Montana leads to the conjecture that spawning runs of Pacific Salmon and/or Steelhead also could have reached this section of the Kootenai River at one time.

QUESTION: Why do some trout have pink flesh while others have white flesh?

ANSWER: Flesh color is related to a trout's diet. Trouts, along with salmons and some other fishes, can extract carotenoid pigmented oils from food and incorporate these oils into the flesh. Crustaceans (for example, water fleas, scuds, and crayfishes) are rich in pigmented oil. Trout with a diet high in crustaceans have pink flesh and salmon-colored eggs; those eating insects and other foods with little or no pigmented oils have white flesh and cream-colored eggs.

QUESTION: What are cold, cool, and warmwater fishes?

ANSWER: Fish are coldblooded—that is, their temperature is about the same as the water surrounding them. This greatly influences their biology and, in turn, their distribution. Members of the trout family are adapted to live in water temperatures lower than 65°F and are examples of coldwater fishes. Sunfishes are known as warmwater fishes. To thrive they must have summer water temperatures of 75°F and higher. Northern Pike, Walleye, and Yellow Perch prefer summer temperatures in the midrange, 65° to 75° F, and have come to be known as coolwater fishes.

QUESTION: What is a char?

ANSWER: Char (also charr) is a name often given to trouts in the genus *Salvelinus*, which Montana are Brook, Bull, and Lake trout. They are readily told from the other trouts (genera *Oncorhynchus* and *Salmo*), for they have a "reversed" foreground-background color scheme. Rainbow, cutthroat, Golden, and Brown trout always have foreground markings (spots) which are darker than the background; chars have a relatively darker background, typically gray, with lighter spots.

ADDITIONAL SOURCES OF INFORMATION
ON MONTANA FISHES

Many readers will desire additional information on Montana fishes. Of the many excellent publications available, the following are particularly pertinent:

The first two books contain information on identification, distribution, breeding, and feeding habits of Montana fishes, and the history of fish collections and introductions into Montana. In addition, Brown presents age and growth data for each species.

Brown, C.J.D. *Fishes of Montana*. Big Sky Books, Montana State University, Bozeman, 1971. 207 pp.

Weisel, George F. *Fish Guide for Intermountain Montana*. Montana State University Press, Missoula, 1957. 88 pp. Out of print, but held by the Montana State Library in Helena; it can be borrowed from a local library through interlibrary loan.

Next is a revised scientific key to the identification of Montana fishes. It serves to update *Fishes of Montana*:

Gould, William R. *Key to the Fishes of Montana*. Biology Department, Montana State University, Bozeman, 1995. 22 pp.

The following three books were written for areas other than Montana, but between them they contain in-depth information on all fishes found in Montana waters except tropical aquarium species.

Baxter, George T. and Michael D. Stone. *Fishes of Wyoming*. Wyoming Game and Fish Department, 1995. 290 pp. Features an excellent color photograph of each species in an underwater setting.

Pflieger, William L. *The Fishes of Missouri*. Missouri Department of Conservation, revised 1991. 343 pp. Has unsurpassed illustrated keys.

Scott, W.B. and E.J. Crossman. *Freshwater Fishes of Canada*. Bulletin 184, Fisheries Research Board of Canada, reprinted with corrections 1985. 966 pp. A tremendous source book—extremely detailed descriptions of individual species plus extensive life history accounts. Includes over 80% of the fishes found in Montana.

LIST OF MONTANA FISHES
(Including selected hybrids)

Families in this list are in phylogenetic order—that is, from the most primitive to the most advanced. Within families the scientific names (genus and species) are listed alphabetically. This is different from the arrangement of fishes throughout this book, which is based on the type and position of fins on the back (see pp. 8-9).

SYMBOLS

N — Native.   I — Introduced.   P — Possibly native.

C — A fish of special concern.

E — Listed as endangered under the federal Endangered Species Act. Retains status as state fish of special concern.

*—Designated a game fish in Montana statutes.

#—Designated a nongame fish in need of management in Administrative Rules of Montana

STURGEON FAMILY - ACIPENSERIDAE
N * E	White Sturgeon	*Acipenser transmontanus*
N * E	Pallid Sturgeon	*Scaphirhynchus albus*
N *	Shovelnose Sturgeon	*Scaphirhynchus platorynchus*

PADDLEFISH FAMILY - POLYODONTIDAE
N * C	Paddlefish	*Polyodon spathula*

GAR FAMILY - LEPISOSTEIDAE
N C	Shortnose Gar	*Lepisosteus platostomus*

MOONEYE FAMILY - HIODONTIDAE
N	Goldeye	*Hiodon alosoides*

MINNOW FAMILY - CYPRINIDAE
I		Goldfish	*Carassius auratus*
N		Lake Chub	*Couesius plumbeus*
I		Common Carp	*Cyprinus carpio*
I		Utah Chub	*Gila atraria*
N		Western Silvery Minnow	*Hybognathus argyritis*
N		Brassy Minnow	*Hybognathus hankinsoni*
N		Plains Minnow	*Hybognathus placitus*
N	C	Sturgeon Chub	*Macrhybopsis gelida*
N	C	Sicklefin Chub	*Macrhybopsis meeki*
N	C	Pearl Dace	*Margariscus margarita*
N		Peamouth	*Mylocheilus caurinus*
I		Golden Shiner	*Notemigonus crysoleucas*
N		Emerald shiner	*Notropis atherinoides*
I		Spottail Shiner	*Notropis hudsonius*
N		Sand Shiner	*Notropis stramineus*
N		Northern Redbelly Dace	*Phoxinus eos*

√	C	Northern Redbelly Dace x Finescale Dace (hybrid)	*Phoxinus eos x P. neogaeus*
√		Fathead Minnow	*Pimephales promelas*
√		Flathead Chub	*Platygobio gracilis*
√		Northern Squawfish	*Ptychocheilus oregonensis*
√		Longnose Dace	*Rhinichthys cataractae*
√		Redside Shiner	*Richardsonius balteatus*
√		Creek Chub	*Semotilus atromaculatus*

UCKER FAMILY - CATOSTOMIDAE

√		River Carpsucker	*Carpiodes carpio*
√		Longnose Sucker	*Catostomus catostomus*
√		White Sucker	*Catostomus commersoni*
√		Largescale Sucker	*Catostomus macrocheilus*
√		Mountain Sucker	*Catostomus platyrhynchus*
√	C	Blue Sucker	*Cycleptus elongatus*
		Smallmouth Buffalo	*Ictiobus bubalus*
		Bigmouth Buffalo	*Ictiobus cyprinellus*
√		Shorthead Redhorse	*Moxostoma macrolepidotum*

ULLHEAD CATFISH FAMILY - ICTALURIDAE

		Black Bullhead	*Ameiurus melas*
		Yellow Bullhead	*Ameiurus natalis*
	*	Channel Catfish	*Ictalurus punctatus*
		Stonecat	*Noturus flavus*

IKE FAMILY - ESOCIDAE

	*	Northern Pike	*Esox lucius*
	*	Tiger Muskellunge (hybrid)	*Esox lucius x E. masquinongy*

UDMINNOW FAMILY - UMBRIDAE

		Central Mudminnow	*Umbra limi*

MELT FAMILY - OSMERIDAE

		Rainbow Smelt	*Osmerus mordax*

ROUT FAMILY - SALMONIDAE

		Cisco	*Coregonus artedi*
		Lake Whitefish	*Coregonus clupeaformis*
		Golden Trout	*Oncorhynchus aguabonita*
	* C	Yellowstone Cutthroat Trout	*Oncorhynchus clarki bouvieri*
	* C	Westslope Cutthroat Trout	*Oncorhynchus clarki lewisi*
		Rainbow Trout	*Oncorhynchus mykiss*
	* C	Redband Trout	*Oncorhynchus mykiss* subspecies
	*	Kokanee	*Oncorhynchus nerka*
		Chinook Salmon	*Oncorhynchus tshawytscha*
	*	Pygmy Whitefish	*Prosopium coulteri*
	*	Mountain Whitefish	*Prosopium williamsoni*
		Brown Trout	*Salmo trutta*
		Tiger Trout (hybrid)	*Salmo trutta x Salvelinus fontinalis*
	* C	Bull Trout	*Salvelinus confluentus*
		Brook Trout	*Salvelinus fontinalis*
	*	Lake Trout	*Salvelinus namaycush*
	*	Arctic Grayling	*Thymallus arcticus*
	* C	Arctic Grayling (fluvial)	*Thymallus arcticus*

TROUT-PERCH FAMILY - PERCOPSIDAE
N   C   Trout-perch   *Percopsis omiscomaycus*

CODFISH FAMILY- GADIDAE
N *   Burbot   *Lota lota*

KILLIFISH FAMILY - CYPRINODONTIDAE
I   Plains Killifish   *Fundulus zebrinus*

LIVEBEARER FAMILY - POECILIIDAE
I   Western Mosquitofish   *Gambusia affinis*
I   Sailfin Molly   *Poecilia latipinna*
I   Shortfin Molly   *Poecilia mexicana*
I   Green Swordtail   *Xiphophorus helleri*
I   Variable Platyfish   *Xiphophorus variatus*

STICKLEBACK FAMILY - GASTEROSTEIDAE
N   Brook Stickleback   *Culaea inconstans*

SCULPIN FAMILY - COTTIDAE
N   Mottled Sculpin   *Cottus bairdi*
N   Slimy Sculpin   *Cottus cognatus*
N   C   Shorthead Sculpin   *Cottus confusus[1]*
N   Torrent Sculpin   *Cottus rhotheus*
N   C   Spoonhead Sculpin   *Cottus ricei*

TEMPERATE BASS FAMILY - PERCICHTHYIDAE
I   White Bass   *Morone chrysops*

SUNFISH FAMILY - CENTRARCHIDAE
I   Rock Bass   *Ambloplites rupestris*
I   Green Sunfish   *Lepomis cyanellus*
I   Pumpkinseed   *Lepomis gibbosus*
I   Bluegill   *Lepomis macrochirus*
I *   Smallmouth Bass   *Micropterus dolomieu*
I *   Largemouth Bass   *Micropterus salmoides*
I #   White Crappie   *Pomoxis annularis*
I #   Black Crappie   *Pomoxis nigromaculatus*

PERCH FAMILY - PERCIDAE
N   Iowa Darter   *Etheostoma exile*
I #   Yellow Perch   *Perca flavescens*
N *   Sauger   *Stizostedion canadense*
I *   Walleye   *Stizostedion vitreum*
I *   Saugeye (hybrid)   *Stizostedion canadense x S. vitreum*

DRUM FAMILY - SCIAENIDAE
N   Freshwater Drum   *Aplodinotus grunniens*

---

[1]***Cottus confusus*** *may be a variant of* **C. bairdi** *(see COMMENT at bottom of p. 86).*

INDEX

Boldface page numbers indicate color illustrations.
See pp. 98-100 for list of scientific names.

STOP!

Do not introduce any fish without authorization from
Montana Fish, Wildlife & Parks.
It is not only the wrong thing to do—it is illegal.

THE PERILS OF ILLEGAL FISH PLANTS

Sport fish populations have been severely damaged or eliminated in almost every lake an
stream where fish have been illegally introduced and there have been more than 295 docu
mented cases of illegal transplants at 181 locations in Montana through 1995. Yellow Perc
have been the most common problem fish. Northern Pike follow in occurrence and damag
done, and even minnows and suckers dumped from bait buckets have caused irretrievabl
damage.

Problems from the new species include voracious predation that decimates existing game
forage fishes, competition for food and space, interbreeding or hybridization with close
related species, introduction of diseases and parasites, and even alteration of the aquatic hab
tat as when Common Carp is introduced.

Sometimes there is a cure. The entire fish population in a relatively small lake can be kill
with chemicals and the lake restocked with desirable species, but this is costly and seldo
feasible. Chemical fish eradication is not attainable in streams, large lakes, or even small lak
that have weed beds, springs, or significant inflow and outflow.

Please help maintain Montana's outstanding fisheries by protecting against illegal fish plan
and helping educate others on its perils.